Achyut Potdar

A Life of Simplicity,
Resilience & Contentment

By Daughter

Anuradha Paraskar

Qurate
quratebooks.com
Because everyone has a story to tell

Achyut Potdar

- A Life of Simplicity, Resilience & Contentment

Anuradha Paraskar

Published in 2024

© Published by

Qurate Books Pvt. Ltd.
Goa 403523, India
www.qauratebooks.com
Tel: 1800-210-6527, Email: info@quratebooks.com

ISBN: 978-93-58987-05-8

Dedicated to:

My late mother, Asha Potdar who was always the strongest pillar of support to my father, and the rest of us.

We love you and miss you, Mamma. You are forever in our hearts.

Preface

This book celebrates the versatile life of my father Achyut Govind Potdar.

A nonagenarian, his nine decades have encompassed varied experiences gathered across four different professions, along with several personal triumphs and debacles, that displayed immense strength, simplicity, resilience, and love.

A simple man, who never engaged in any kind of self-publicity or PR, he truly deserves a name embossed in the sands of time. While he never really reached the pinnacle of success in the professions he undertook (much as he truly deserved it), I am proud to say that he has certainly achieved excellence in every thing that he did.

My father attributes this largely to the luck factor. However, I believe that my father's simplicity of thinking and living, his acute candor, and his highest level of integrity in thoughts, words, and actions may have eclipsed all the diplomacy, tact,and flattery often needed to take one to greater heights.

Whilst his life journey is unique, given that he could practice four distinct professions, his single greatest passion in life has always been acting. It has always been the truest love of his life. Even today at 90, his face lights up if he is asked to act. I sense that his highest joy, peace, and contentment comes from when he is enacting a role – when he gets fully absorbed in a character.

I am a blessed daughter, as my father has been staying with me ever since my mother's demise in May, 2019. When he moved here, he brought with him all the files and diaries that he had created over the years.

One day, I noticed a beautiful white file amongst all his other well-maintained files. It is a neatly made file in which in his beautiful handwriting, reminiscent of neatly arranged pearls, he has listed down all his work in films, television serials, advertisements, and theatre. He has also documented all his financial contributions made across the country to over 70 institutions to promote Marathi youth in arts and culture. It's a unique feat for a man to contribute all his earnings made through acting toward the encouragement of others. Everything is systematically listed in chronological order, highlighted in different colors – a habit he consistently maintains to this day. He has titled this file "SAMADHAAN: The Joy of Giving". The contents of this file surprised me with how silently he has done so much work, over and above his job, and yet never made any mention of it even to the family. My eyes couldn't help but well up with love and pride.

I realize that his needs have been minimal and he has always been very kind. He gives away without blinking an eyelid. Perhaps, the most unique gesture he may have made so naturally was when he gave a cheque to his TV serial producers during Covid. A set of new and very young producers were making the *Maza Hoshil Na* TV serial for Zee Marathi. He played the patriarch Appa in this serial. During Covid, he told them that they would have fixed costs of hiring the set even though shooting had stopped. He contributed towards these costs. The young team was overwhelmed by this thoughtful and generous gesture. They did not encash the cheque, but framed it as a mark of respect, and kept it in their office.

My father tells me that he was never very ambitious, but whatever he did in the past 90 years in any profession or even in general life, was with the fullest level of sincerity, hard work, and devotion. He says he always put his best effort into everything he did, with the highest level of integrity and ethos. Today when he reflects on his life, it is this value system that he gives credit to for the immense peace and contentment in his life.

At 90, when I ask him how he would sum up his life in one word, he smiles and says he has "SAMADHAAN." *Samadhaan*, in our mother tongue Marathi means contentment.

He is extremely quiet and at peace with himself, today. He never complains nor troubles anyone with any demands or expectations. A typical day in his life today involves solving the daily Marathi crossword in Maharashtra Times newspaper with 100 percent accuracy, playing the card game Solitaire by himself for an hour, watching India TV news with two pegs of Old Monk rum, and spending the rest of his time lying down on his bed and resting. Always a disciplined man, his meals, going down for a ride in his wheelchair, and his sleep time are all set to the clock.

I think my father has truly lived a full life. Our father is our hero. I am indeed honored to get an opportunity to write this book about him. The love and respect he has received from one and all cannot be captured in a single book. In the last chapter of this book *Hearts Touched,* I have included various quotes from people who know and love him.

The story behind the book

As a daughter who spent over three decades in the marketing and media world, my late husband Shirish would always ask me why I couldn't swing an interview in Filmfare or Stardust or get some TV channel to interview my father. He was doing several significant roles in films, serials, and theatre in those days. People recognized his face and loved his natural acting, but most fans did not know his name. Publicity and media coverage would have certainly helped him develop a deeper connection with the audience and perhaps opened the doors to bigger acting opportunities.

But being my father's daughter with the highest ethos of not leveraging my position for any personal gains, I could never find it in myself to do that. There is still that regret that remains in my mind about never having found a way to promote my father without compromising on my integrity and ethos. So in 2018, after I left the corporate world and started my consulting practice, I floated the idea of a short film that would remain on YouTube and serve as a biopic, keeping him in public memory for the years to come. My siblings Amrish and Aparna, joyfully agreed.

We rushed into getting the short film made. It was directed by a young new Director Anup Choudhary, who was introduced to me by my sister Aparna's husband Govind. The reason for the rush was my ailing mother who was terminally ill with lung cancer and had little time left. We wanted her to feature in his life's biopic as she was truly the wind beneath his wings. We shot the film quickly in my home and my building compound at Thane over two days.

We circulated the link to this short 10-minute film to all our contacts through WhatsApp on 6th May 2019 which was our parents' 57th wedding anniversary. Sadly, my mother passed away on 7th May, the very next day. She saw the film but was so weak that I am not sure how much she could absorb or appreciate.

You can see this short film on YouTube, titled ***Achyut Potdar: Celeb documentary***

Time flew. Often when I heard my father narrate incidents from his life, especially the ones on film sets, to people when he was in the mood, I would think about writing them down and publishing a book about him. But I never really got down to it.

Recently in Feb 2024, he got seriously unwell and nearly collapsed. We admitted him to the nearby Jupiter hospital. Fortunately, my father, who is like a cat blessed with nine lives, bounced back. However, this time it was with a lot of weakness in his back and lower limbs. The heart was already weak. Shooting was now an impossible thing to do. All his siblings and peers had passed away and his beloved wife and dearest and nearest friend Narayan Joshi were no more. All this affected the independent and active man that he always has been, and he started feeling low. He instructed us in February 2024 that if he did get unwell again, we should refrain from hospitalization and simply let him go.

His cardiologist Dr. Rane started treating him at home since February 2024, after he expressed his desire to not be admitted to the hospital ever again.

During one of his visits, the Doctor suggested to my father to write an autobiography, as it would keep him busy and motivated if he reminisced and wrote about his life. I realized that if my father did this, it would also be an excellent read for people to know more about the man they had often seen on screen and invariably exclaimed "What a fine actor!"

It was agreed that I would sit down daily with him and jot down notes and pen them down in the first person for him as his autobiography. But I realized (and painfully so) in this last month since I started writing, that my father who has always been blessed with a telescopic memory, has grown old rapidly in the last few months. He could hardly remember the *kissas* (incidents) he would speak of in earlier days. In fact, with his flair for writing and fine command over language, he would have needed no one to write for him.

I guess this whole project is perhaps 5 years late. Somewhere during our daily writing sessions, my father suggested that instead of penning it down as his autobiography, I should be the author. I realized that there was merit in his suggestion because if I wrote it, I could say several things about his person and character that he would have, perhaps, not said himself.

I am not a regular writer and have never really written anything before. I do hope I have done justice to his simple life and character, and I hope you find this an engaging read.

I wish to thank everyone who contributed in small and big ways with their experiences and memories created with my father over the last 9 decades.

Sincerely,

Anuradha

22nd August, 2024

(his Ninetieth birthday)

Contents

1
Origins of a legacy: From Jabalpur to Indore

My father was born in Jabalpur, Madhya Pradesh in a middle-class Karhade Brahmin Marathi family, to Shri Govindrao Krishnarao Potdar and Smt. Radhabai Govindrao Potdar. He was the 10th child after two brothers and three sisters and 4 infantile deaths. After him, another brother was born.

My father's birthday was listed as 16th October 1934 in school, but at home, they always celebrated it as per *tithi,* which was two days before the Rakhi festival. It was several years later that we found out that this day corresponded to 22nd August in the year 1934 and it's only in the last 3 decades that we have been celebrating both days in our family.

The family traces its origins to Karad, near Satara in Maharashtra, but they had migrated to Indore and other central provinces at least two generations earlier. Probably they would have been part of several thousand Brahmin families that moved from Maharashtra along with Maratha rulers in the 19th century. Indore, Gwalior

Jhansi, and Baroda are places where you will still find a huge population of Maharashtrian Brahmins settled down the generations.

The original surname of my father's family was Orpe. There is no knowledge available on when they changed it to Potdar. Potdar was a position that was given to the person who collected revenue tax from peasants, deposited it in the royal treasury, and gave receipts to the peasants. In this case, probably some great-grandfather must have served as a Potdar with a royal family somewhere.

Incidentally, when one traces back the family tree, Padmabhushan Shri Datto Waman Potdar, the famous historian, writer orator, and Vice-chancellor of Pune University was also a part of our Potdar clan.

My grandfather Govindrao Potdar, a tall man with a lean physique, carried an aura of strictness in his demeanor. He had studied up to class 8 and worked in the Indian railways, which gave him a lot of transfers and postings. In one such posting at Jabalpur, my father was born as the 10th offspring. Starting as a clerk, Govindrao retired as a CTC, Chief Traffic Canvasser. Surface transport had just started in those days and Railways had started losing revenue. His position as a CTC involved marketing the Railways to clients for their cargo shipments.

Govindrao had one brother Sadashivrao who had two sons, Gajanan and Dr Keshav. Gajanan Potdar was a freedom fighter and a close ally of Chandrashekhar Azad, Bhagatsingh and Rajguru. He was a freedom fighter. I am told that he used to secretly make bombs in the college laboratory with his friends and supply them to other freedom fighters. He went to jail several times during the Independence movement and later settled in Mumbai to work in the film industry as a scriptwriter. He was also a journalist writing news and reviews. Gajanan Potdar known as Nana, lived in Dadar at Mumbai and often visited us in his later years when we lived at Mahim. At that age, I had no idea of the amazing feats of this freedom fighter in the pre-independence era. Dr Keshav Potdar, the other son, was a practicing medical Doctor settled in Karol Bagh Delhi. He was a very jovial man. I have memories of visiting his place as a child and enjoying his magnanimous hospitality and laughter.

My grandmother Radhabai Potdar came from Vidisha, near Bhopal. Daughter of a zamindar, she was just 12 when she married Govindrao. There are tales that I have heard from my aunt that she was from a wealthy

Parents

With cousin Sadashiv and brother Madhav

family and when she got married, she was weighed on a scale and that much weight of silver, money, gifts, dry fruits, and sweets was gifted to her. Known as Bitiya in her maternal home, she had two brothers, Martandrao Nawathe, who had 5 daughters and one son, and Jageshwarrao Nawathe who did not marry. My father has very faint memories of going to Vidisha as a child, but he vividly remembers the presence of a *tope* (cannon) in that house.

Radhabai was gifted with medical acumen. Despite being educated only up to class 4, she had a knack for curing diseases like jaundice and malaria with her household naturopathy medicines. She would have this plywood box that had all kinds of herbs and people in the neighborhood trusted her for helping them in times of need. She also had the skills of a very good midwife and was always sought after for assisting ladies in their complex deliveries at home. She would do all this free of cost. An interesting facet of the lady was that being a Railway employee's wife, she knew the railway timetable by heart. I am told that she could easily and simply rattle off train names with their arrival and departure times at Indore.

Govindrao and Radhabai had eleven children of which 7 survived beyond infancy. The eldest son was Ramchandra Potdar, who left education to become a freedom fighter. After independence, he worked in the Railways for some time. He later started a few businesses and finally became a tutor in Pinge‘s classes at Dadar Mumbai. He was also a poet.

Their next son was Madhav Potdar, perhaps the brightest of all siblings and most entrepreneurial. He did his Bachelor's in commerce with a first class first from Lucknow University. He had successful businesses like steel furniture and flour mills, and in those days, he was so stylish and successful that he drove an imported car. However, he later wound up all businesses and dedicated himself to becoming an avid disciple of Akkalkot Swami Gajanan Maharaj. Agnihotra practice leads to healthy life, became his motto and he opened an Ashram on the outskirts of Bhopal at Bairagadh. This Ashram still thrives and is called Madhavashram, from where he had started preaching and teaching Agnihotra. His three daughters run it today.

Family

With sisters Ambika and Suman

Then came three daughters Durga, Ambika, and Suman. The girls were blessed to receive a good education in those days and all of them knew cycling. Durga and Ambika played excellent badminton and the latter even knew horse riding. All of them became teachers in schools and the youngest daughter Suman rose to become the principal of a girl's school in Indore.

On the back of the 3 girls, another son was born - my father Achyut Potdar. This was followed by another son Vasant, who was a popular writer of books in Bengali, Marathi, and Hindi on varied subjects. He staged one-man shows narrating the freedom struggle called Vande Mataram all over India and abroad.

■ ■ ■

2

Early childhood and a father's teachings

My father was born on 22nd August 1934 in Jabalpur. This was his father's last posting before retirement. The eldest sister Durga had just got married into a family in Indore, prompting their father to move to Indore in 1940, after his retirement and six years in Jabalpur. My father's only memory of the Jabalpur home is that of being spanked for eating a laundry soap bar that he mistook for a sweet made by his eldest sister Durga.

At Indore, they first moved into a rented house near Ganesh Mandir. It was a three-room tenement with all three rooms side by side like in a railway bogie. My father was admitted to the upper primary school in Khajuri bazaar area which was very near his home. He did his classes 3 and 4 from this school. It was a typical yesteryear school where the children sat on a *chatai* and wore a traditional dress of shirt shorts and a *topi* with chappal. There was no uniform and the teacher taught on a blackboard. He was moved to Maharaja Shivajirao Marathi Middle School for classes 5 to 8.

Finally, in Dec 1942, the family moved to their own home, a newly constructed building with two storeys, in an area called Martand Chowk at Indore. It seems my grandfather had invested in some silver *paats*, low-height stools on which people sit,at the time of his daughters' weddings. He sold them off and raised some 15000 rupees to make this home after he retired from the Railways. The 2000 square feet plot was purchased in a simple residential neighborhood of Martand Chowk, near the *Rajwada* in central Indore. Fifty percent of the residents here were Maharashtrians. The family named it Radha Niwas. Radha was my grandmother's name.

The house had six rooms on the ground floor, five rooms on the first floor, and four rooms on the second floor. Intricately designed balconies made the home look elegant, and it stood out in Martand Chowk. A lot of wood was used in its construction. There were three toilets in the backyard because, in those days, toilets were always constructed outside the house. There was a large verandah on the ground floor which had a *Tulsi Vrindavan.* There were two small terraces on the second floor. Additionally, there were two cellars in the basement.

Radha Niwas, Indore

22 Martand Chowk remains a Potdar home even today.

The family started living a simple and happy life in

their new home. My grandfather was my father's ideal. He taught my father the values of simple living and high thinking. He imbibed in him the value of Guru worship at a very young age. He remembers when he was in class 3, his father would call his class teacher Naik Sir to their home on Dussehra day and make my father worship him. He would then gift the teacher a towel or a shawl as *Guru Dakshina*. These values of Guru worship remained with my father forever.

Father Govindrao

My grandfather was a strict disciplinarian. Everything had to be like clockwork and no deviations were allowed. Once when my father was in class 5 and had slightly overspent his sanctioned play time at his friend Arun

Playing violin

Date's house, my grandfather held him by the ear and got him home with the earlobe held tight in his fingers. The pain lasted a few days, but the lesson stayed for years.

In early 1945, my grandfather Govindrao took ill. He was afflicted with asthma and passed away on 7th April 1945 at the Radha Niwas residence. My father was in class 6 then. On that day, he was late in getting back home, as his teacher had kept him back in class to assist him after school. My father was his favorite and most trusted student. Being a very young boy, the elders did not call him back from school and when he reached home, the funeral procession had already left. To this day, he regrets not having had one last glimpse of his father. His innocence was such that he did not realize what he had lost. In some ways, there was a childlike joy that lingered. A strict father would no longer be there to trouble him. In the 10-day mourning period called *sutak*, my father and his brother would often find some coins lying here and there in the house and would go buy some *nariyal paak* sweets from the nearby fruit market shop.

■ ■ ■

3

His first Guru: Tai, his mother

My father's mother was his first Guru. She was called Tai at home. She was a typical loving and caring mother but there was a strictness to her too. A very pious lady, she did lots of rituals which included doing pooja every day, celebrating festivals like *Ganeshotsav* and *Navratri* in the fullest tradition, *Kumarika bhojan* every Friday, *Sawashni bhojan and Bramhan bhojan* during Navratri, and everything that a typical Maharashtrian Brahmin household would do. Every morning at 8 am, a Brahmin would come for the daily pooja at home and he would be given a glass of milk after the pooja was done. The family had the

Mother Radhabai

typical culture of sitting down on a *paat* and eating food after taking god's name and reciting a shloka. Their day started and ended with the recitation of shlokas. Every evening, they had to recite *Ramraksha, Bheemroopi*, and 21 other shlokas. They had to also recite *parvacha*, all mathematics tables, before sleeping. Touching the feet of all seniors daily was also a ritual.

My father however had religion-agnostic tendencies since childhood and he did not like the daily rituals. He narrates how he would sometimes just casually spill off the water during the *Sandhya pooja* and how his mother would watch from behind the curtain and then spank him.

Radhabai was a very good cook and would get delicious treats made during festivals. Simple vegetarian food was the usual fare at home. There would be no onion garlic in *Chaturmaas* and every Monday and Saturday would be *upwaas* fare. My father simply loved the *sabudana khichdi* and *shingadyacha shira* made on those *upwaas* days.

Being a large family, childbirths were a frequent occurrence in the *balantinichi kholi*, the maternity room at Radha Niwas. Unlike all other rooms that had tiles, this special room was kept rustic and was smoothened with cow dung regularly. The logic was to keep it sterile and antiseptic as several deliveries were done in this room. This room in later years became my grandmother's bedroom and eventually my aunt Akka's bedroom. My father fondly recalls that, due to the regular arrivals of new babies of the daughters or nieces, the house was always well-stocked with delicious and nutritious items like *dinkache ladoo, methiche ladoo, aleevache ladoo, and aale paak* during the winters. These were all made in large quantities and stored in three big containers, one for the lady who had delivered and the other two for guests and family members. My father has fond memories of these goodies

The home was always brimming with people visiting my grandmother, especially her older children with their families. All the daughters would come visiting in vacations with their children and there used to be a lot of family bonding because of the large house. My grandmother's brother and his family lived on the ground floor and his family was very large too. One daughter Ambika Kibe resided on the second floor with her husband and six children whilst the Potdars resided on the first floor.

She was a social person and had a large network of people she engaged with. All girls in Indore who called her *kaku or mami or maushi* became her dear ones. In Adhik maas, all their husbands therefore became her deemed sons-in-law. She would organize to make a sweet called *Anarse,* lay 33 each in 33 big silver plates, and get them distributed to these sons-in-law. Once a cousin of mine asked her if someone was a second cousin. My grandmother said there is no first or second or cousin. All are brothers and sisters. Earlier when they were in Jabalpur, and if they were invited to any young boy's *Munja* ceremony, she would gift the boy a gold *kardoda,* a waist chain. In those years, she would often have seven to eight *ashrit* people living in her home. They were often orphans or poor boys to whom she gave shelter and

food. In later years, when she was seriously unwell and nearing her death, she organized to buy several nine-yard sarees and stacked them in a cupboard by her bedside. She would gift a saree to every woman who visited her in those days. Such was her kind approach and ability to give. My father imbibed this trait from his mother, as you will learn in a later chapter.

Radhabai was a brave and smart lady. When her husband passed away, her two youngest sons Achyut and Vasant were just eleven and nine years old. Therefore her bond with them grew even stronger. She made sure they were well cared for and raised to be kind, responsible individuals. My father was deeply attached to his mother. He would lie next to her for five minutes each night, right up to her last days. Even after getting married, he continued this practice before going to his bedroom. Every night, he would press his mother's feet as a mark of love and respect. He has always believed that our home, Radha Niwas, is his temple and his mother the goddess. From then on, he needed no other idols to worship.

My father would walk to school with his friends from the neighborhood. He got his first cycle after passing class 10, a cherished milestone. Back then, there was no radio in the house and entertainment meant doing *gupshup* with friends or playing games like *gillidanda, dabba aaispais, kanche, lingorcha*, cards, carrom, and cricket. For cricket, he would buy second-hand broken bats for 2 rupees from the Yeshwant Club and balls for 25 paise.

There was no system of breakfast in those days, so it was always about coming back home to eat home-cooked meals. Occasionally during the summer, his mother would hire an ice cream pot and make ice cream at home, which was an unlimited delight for the young boys. Round the year, my grandmother also would keep large brass containers stocked with *murmura chiwda, shankarpale, besan ladoos, and sattu* for all her children, grandchildren, and visitors to eat

Summer vacations would have large gatherings of children and grandchildren and popular card games like *Rummy and Laalpaan satti* were the routine entertainment. Occasionally my grandmother would permit her grandchildren to see a movie like *Chhoti Behan* or any movie with a clean storylineIn those days, Indore city had this concept of large tents selling sugarcane juice and they were all called *Madhushala.* Occasionally the boys would get money to go and drink sugarcane juice from the *Madhushala* near their home

Such was the simple and joyful lifestyle of his childhood, under the strong influence of his mother. The family had a lady who would come to make rotis and one maid called Sitabai who was their household help. Their salaries were rupees one and three per month respectively.

■ ■ ■

4

At School, he found his second Guru

My father was a very sincere student with a remarkable telescopic memory, allowing him to memorize textbooks by heart. In one memorable incident in class 5, he received only 33 marks on his history paper and his father spanked him for getting such low marks. Crying, he insisted that he wrote everything correctly and even narrated some of the answers to his father. Shocked, his father hugged him and rushed to school. When they confronted the

teacher, she admitted that all his answers were exactly as written in the textbook and hence she had inferred that the boy had cheated. Proudly, my grandfather challenged the teacher to ask his son to recite any of the 120 pages from the History book. To everyone's astonishment, my father could recite any page of the book with precise punctuation. Both the teacher and the principal apologized for wrongly accusing him of cheating.

The senior boys in the school came to know of this feat and they would often admiringly and jovially ask my father to recite a page number and he would gladly oblige them. Guess this gift of memory proved invaluable later in his theatre pursuits where long dialogues were the order of the day!

In those days, children were not allowed to watch films. The circus was the only entertainment permitted, and it came to Indore either annually or once every two to three years. The only film children were allowed to see in the cinema hall was *Ramrajya*. However, my father

and his friends often heard a lot of Hindi film songs played at sugarcane stalls or during wedding baraats(processions) passing through the streets. One song that became extremely popular in those days was the song *Aana meri jaan meri jaan Sunday ke Sunday* from the film Shehnai. It was played everywhere in Indore. There was a line in that song that said A*aa tujhe London dikhaoo.* But this line would cost my father dearly. The story goes as follows.

One day in his Marathi class at school, the children were learning about punctuation. The teacher demonstrated how breaking a sentence with commas at different points could change its meaning. In a mischievous mood, my father, recalling the song, jokingly asked his neighboring student if the line *Aa tujhe London dikhaoo* could be punctuated differently. The teacher caught the boys giggling and punished them by making them stand like *murgas* all day!

In class 7, his mother appointed Pol Master as his Mathematics tutor. Pol Master came home daily to teach my father Mathematics, and thanks to his excellent guidance, my father secured full marks, 100/100 in his Matriculation exam. For this achievement, my father received a cash prize of Rs. 10 and a Marathi book titled *Swarajya Margadarshak* by Lokmanya Tilak from the school.

My father regards Pol Master as the second Guru of his life, crediting him for making a challenging subject like Mathematics as soft as butter. A simple man with a passion for teaching, he was regarded as the best Mathematics teacher in Indore in those days. Later, my father realized that his wife was distantly related to Pol Master, as he was the brother-in-law of her paternal aunt. Every time my father visited Indore, he made it a point to visit Pol Master's house to touch his feet and seek his blessings. Pol Master always lovingly told everyone that my father was his favorite student. Later, my father put my brother through Mathematics tuition with Pol Master as he was rather weak in the subject.

Pol Master passed away in 2017 at age 94, leaving behind fond memories.

■■■

5

Graduation, new pursuits, and the seeds of theatre

After his superb performance in Matriculation, my father's academic performance declined during his college years. He attended Holkar College for the 11th and 12th classes, known as Intermediate in those days. He then pursued a B. Sc. in Physics, Chemistry, and Mathematics, which was a two-year course at the time. While he cleared B. Sc. (Prev), he took a break before appearing for B. Sc. (Final). During this one-year gap, he worked as a Mathematics teacher for 5th to 8th classes, at the Marathi Middle School where he had studied. The reasons he cites for his reduced interest and lower scores in B. Sc were distraction and lack of focus, coupled with a growing interest

in theatre. The renowned Marathi playwright and author, Padmavibhushan Shri P. L. Deshpande, had visited Indore then, becoming both a distraction and an inspiration for my father.

The story unfolds in 1953, during his second and final year of B. Sc. My father was elected Secretary of the Marathi Literary Association of Holkar College. The Association had an annual budget of only Rs. 250, insufficient for the various activities that the young men had planned. Hence, they decided to screen the newly released Hindi film *Anhonee* as a fundraiser and in the process raised a little over Rs.750. With this money, they could afford to invite the Marathi literary genius Shri P. L. Deshpande as Chief guest for their annual function and sponsor his railway ticket to and from Indore to Mumbai. Their teacher, Professor Jadhav of Holkar College personally went to invite the Chief Guest.

With Pu La Deshpande at extreme right

Pu La as he was affectionately and popularly known, came to Indore planning to stay for just 2 days. To save costs, it was decided that he would put up in my father's residence Radha Niwas. However, *Pu La* fell so in love with Indore and its people, that he extended his stay to 15 days. My father's younger brother Vasant became *Pu La's* man Friday during this time.

Every day numerous people flocked to Radha Niwas to meet *Pu La*, and the house buzzed with lively sessions. Simply hearing *Pu La* recite his anecdotes, articles, and plays, mesmerized my young father. These interactions ignited his passion for theatre and acting, profoundly influencing his interests and aspirations. There was lots of *khana peena* and *hasee majaak* every day. Indori *poha* and *mawa jalebi* were *Pu La's* favorite foods. He slept in the guest room, which later became my father's bedroom after his marriage. I am told that *Pu La* completed the writing of his famous play *Tuza aahe Tuzpaashi* in those 2 weeks at Indore at our house.

Meanwhile, the Marathi Literary Association of Holkar College organized *Pu La's* lectures and sessions at various Institutes like Ahilyashram School, Medical College, Christian College, Gujarati College, etc., raising additional funds in the process. At that time, unlike in Maharashtra, *Pu La* was less known in Indore, especially to the non-Marathi audiences. In one incident at the Medical college, when he began speaking on the stage, some students started hooting sh sh sh ...*Pu La* in his classical witty style asked my father if this was a medical college or a Shoemakers college.

After two weeks, *Pu La* left for Bihar with Kumar Gandharvaji for another tour. The impact on my young father was long-lasting. He says that he got so inspired and mesmerized by *Pu La* that he entered a dream world filled with art and theatre. Consequently, his interest in B. Sc. subjects declined drastically, leading to poor academic performance. He had hardly studied during this critical year of B. Sc. (Final).My father chose to take a break from his studies and pursue a career as a Mathematics teacher in Middle school earning a modest salary of Rs. 54 per month in the pay scale grade 30-1-40. His brother-in-law Shri Prabhakar Kibe who was an English teacher in High school helped him get this job.

During this time, he developed an aspiration to join the Indian Air Force as a fighter pilot and applied for the position in 1954. Unfortunately, he was disqualified on medical grounds because his blood showed traces of albumin which was a strict no-no for pilots. That dream remained unfulfilled.

By March 1955, he still felt unprepared to complete his B. Sc. final exams, having devoted much of his time to teaching. He took a drop once again. His older brother Madhavji Potdar, who was called Anna in the family, then took him to Bhopal as an understudy. Anna was around 24 years older than my father and hence was a father figure to him and there was a level of fear driven by respect. He stayed with his brother's family for a year and would go daily to his brother's office which was opposite Bhopal Talkies on Hamidiya Road. The job given to him was to assist Anna's secretary Mr. Quamar in his day-to-day work for the steel furniture business. After a year in Bhopal with his brother's family, my father's experience was far from ideal. His sister-in-law was indifferent, and his brother had little time for him,

Brother Anna (Madhavji)

leaving him feeling uncomfortable and out of place. He felt awkward and thus returned to Indore. He then started working for Anna in his flour mills business in Indore. The company was called Central India Flour Mills, and it was based in Bhopal. The task assigned to my father was to study the Indore market, find out the competitive rates in the commodity market, and write a letter daily to his brother giving the data he had collected. The letter would arrive on the third day at Bhopal. This was a demanding job, and he did not find time to study. The Mathematics in B. Sc. (Final) was not easy. The time had come for him to turn around completely and focus on his studies.

He stopped working for his brother and took up another job as a teacher at Malharashram High School. This was in the pay scale 40-3-70. The job timings were 8.30 to 11.30 am and 2.30 to 4.30 pm. My father remained determined to complete his B. Sc. He made a strategic decision to switch from Mathematics to Economics, focusing intensely on his studies. His hard work paid off, and in 1957, he successfully passed his B. Sc. (Final) exams.

Throughout his life, he has demonstrated a resilient spirit, always emerging from setbacks with a determination to succeed, and consistently achieving remarkable success.

6

Medals and the university experience

In 1959, my father with renewed determination, decided to pursue postgraduation. He approached the Principal of his school Mr. Lalge requesting permission to pursue an MA in Economics alongside his teaching duties. To his delight, his request was granted. His daily routine became demanding yet disciplined. He woke up at 6 am, arrived at college by 7 am, and spent the hour in the library taking notes up to 8 am. This is because

Teacher at Malharashram school

the Professor wanted students to take notes from foreign authors' articles and books and get them to his class. From 8 am to 10 am, he would attend lectures before rushing to Malharashram school to teach his first Mathematics class at 10.45 am. He also supervised students during their lunch break. It was a busy schedule however he was grateful for the opportunity that Principal Lalge had given him.

In the afternoon, after teaching more Mathematics classes, he returned home by 5 pm to begin studying for his MA exams. Dinner would be at 8 pm when his new friend from college Avinash (Balu) Shekdar would join him. Both would study up to late hours till midnight and Balu would frequently stay over, returning home early in the morning to freshen up before meeting my father again at 7 am in the library. Such was the hard work and dedication put in by these youngsters, which yielded my father a second rank in the University in MA (Previous) examinations. He made another good friend whilst doing his MA called Radhu Mucchal. Radhu later

went on to run his large family business whilst Balu became an Air Force officer.

My father passed his MA final standing first class first and got the Vikram University medal for the same. There was thus a massive turnaround in his performance after some delays at the graduation level.

This was also the time when the handsome young man had several girls falling for him. Yes, he was chased by girls in college and the neighborhood, and the shy man always ducked the girls by running out from the back door of Radha Niwas. One Sardarni girl who had come to visit the family living in the opposite building had proposed to him without even knowing him. She would stop him on the road and say "*hum bhi pade hai raahon mein, kabhi humein bhi dekh liya karo.*"(meaning " I am here, at least give me a look")He says he would avoid her by going to his violin class from the back door and this became a subject of humor in family and friends ever since. My father says he was extremely clear in his thoughts and was ready only for an arranged marriage which was approved by his family. Hence the question of having any relationship or fling with any girl never even crossed his mind. He proudly says that he remained a one-woman man all his life.

■■■

7

Finding the "One Woman"

The year was 1961. His outstanding performance in MA (Economics) got him a promotion. After a government job at Malharashram school in Indore, he landed another government job at TRS College in Rewa, Madhya Pradesh as a lecturer in Economics. Initially, life at Rewa began as a paying guest at his student Surendra Tiwari's house. He then became a paying guest at Prof Saxena's and then at Professor Neema's house. Finally, before eventually renting a small house in preparation

With Prof. Neema at Rewa College

for his impending marriage, which his family had begun actively arranging.

In the meanwhile, his elder sister Suman (Akka) had returned to Indore after a challenging three-year marriage. The story goes that one day in 1956, Anna the older brother came to Indore with a prospect for Akka. My father says that for some reason, he sensed something wrong with that man, who he felt was not only unimpressive but also unduly shy and indifferent. He was avoiding eye contact with everyone and looked very uncomfortable. However, my father hesitated in expressing his apprehensions to his brother Anna and the marriage took place. It was unfortunate that after three long years at her marital home in Gondia near Nagpur, my aunt gathered the courage to tell her sister that her husband had been indifferent to her and had not consummated the marriage due to a medical issue. That era was different, where girls did not complain but my aunt could not sustain being in a marriage where there was zero communication with her husband.

Since my grandmother was progressive, she asked her daughter to return. A divorce was soon granted by the Indore Family Court on the grounds of a null and void marriage. My aunt remained single till her death at age 90 in November 2018. My father always regrets his lack of taking a stand, at the right time which could have prevented her from that misery. The impact of this incident on his young mind was very high, instilling deep empathy and respect for women. He did not want to see several girls and reject them, which was the norm with arranged marriages. So, he requested the family to assess any potential match for him thoroughly before he met the girl.

His eldest brother's wife Kamalabai was distantly related to my mother and she had put forward this proposal for my father. My mother's family lived in Jhansi, Uttar Pradesh. Jhansi is an hour's drive from Gwalior and hence is very close to the MP border.

My mother hailed from a distinguished family in Jhansi, Uttar Pradesh, with a rich legacy of service and leadership. The Dhulekar family, who had migrated from Dhule in Maharashtra three generations ago, played a significant role in the region. Notably, my great-granduncle, Shri Raghunath Vinayak Dhulekar, was a revered freedom fighter and Member of Parliament. He was instrumental in establishing the Bundelkhand Ayurvedic College in Jhansi and was a staunch supporter of Netaji Subhash Chandra Bose. He maintained close ties with leaders like Dr. Rajendra Prasad, Mahatma Gandhi, and Pandit Nehru during the struggle for Independence. My mother's grandfather Shri Damodar Vinayak Dhulekar was Dean of the Ayurvedic College at Benaras Hindu University, and her father Shri Vishnu Damodar Dhulekar was the Principal of Bundelkhand Ayurvedic College at Jhansi. My grandmother was a gold

His in-laws

medalist from Benaras Hindu University in Ayurvedic medicine.

In 1962, my father visited Jhansi with his eldest sister, Durga Athale, to meet my mother, Ashalata Dhulekar, who was just 20 years old at the time. She was preparing for her BA finals, which were scheduled two months later. My father and mother instantly liked each other, and the wedding date was set for the auspicious day of Akshay Tritiya, on 6th May 1962 at Jhansi. Courtship was unheard of in those days, but my father says they exchanged a few letters in the 4 months leading to their wedding. Before their marriage, my father had apprised my mother that his mother and his sister were very important to him and that she had to give them all the respect they deserved. She

honored his advice from day one. Known for her calm, composed demeanor, my mother effortlessly integrated beautifully into the verbose and dominating Potdar family.

The story of the wedding day goes as follows.

On 5th May 1962, a tenant at Radha Niwas, Mr. Chaskar had organized a bus from Indore to Jhansi for twenty-five people. However, for some unknown reason, both he and the bus vanished, forcing the *baraatis* to take one train to Bhopal first and then change into another train to reach Jhansi. Despite the initial hiccup, they received a very warm welcome from the Dhulekars upon their arrival. The wedding ceremony took place in the courtyard of my mother's maternal home at 36, Pachkuiyya Jhansi. A shamiana was set up to extend the courtyard, accommodating numerous local guests from the Dhulekar family who attended the celebrations. The *baraat* left with the bride on the same night to reach Indore on 7th May. That evening, a dinner was hosted at Ganesh Mandal in Indore for the Potdar family guests to conclude the wedding festivities

Wedding day, 6th May 1962

At Jhansi with his in-laws

The new bride with her In-laws

There was no honeymoon, as my grandmother was unwell, and my father decided to stay back with her till his college vacation was over. May and June 1962 were spent by the newly wedded couple at their home in Radha Niwas, Indore. My father went back to Rewa by the end of June and my mother joined him a month later. My uncle's friend Mr. Chaube escorted her from Indore to Rewa. Those were the early days of marriage, where my father says he spent more time studying and preparing for his lectures on advanced Economics than romancing his young wife. My mother's simplicity and understanding nature provided him with immense strength to face the challenges that lay ahead. Her unassuming demeanor and lack of demands allowed him to focus on his academic and professional responsibilities with renewed vigor.

■■■

8

Into the Indian Army: Captaining wars and plays

In December 1962, just six months after marriage, my father came across an advertisement in the newspaper where the Government was inviting youth to join the Armed Forces. The 1962 China war had just got over and Pakistan had already started brewing trouble. My father had always silently dreamt of a career in the Armed Forces and had been rejected in 1955 by the Indian Air Force on medical grounds. Patriotism was embedded in him, influenced by the legacy of freedom fighters in both his and my mother's families. He discussed his desire to apply for the Army job with my mother and she was supportive and asked him to pursue his dream. Undoubtedly, silently my mother would have worried about letting her husband go into war but being the woman she was, she let my father do what gave him joy. She always strongly supported all his endeavors.

My father applied and appeared for the Jabalpur SSB (Services Selection Board) qualification rounds and was selected. The remarks on his medical certificate were

that he was slightly flat-footed, but which could be managed. Usually, the medical criteria are very strictly adhered to, and even a slight deviation is not allowed. This was thus a testimony to how much the Government needed personnel given the impending Pak war of 1965. Most youth were hesitant to join the Armed forces in those days, after the 2 World Wars and the Indo-China War of 1962.

It was one of the happiest moments of his life to be selected as an Officer in the Indian Army.

Training started in April 1963 at Dehradun. My mother left for Indore from Rewa to stay with my grandmother. The training was hard. Once, they had to run 10 km in a specified time of two hours, in which my father and some others got delayed by a few minutes. This was mainly because he had a flat foot syndrome affecting his running speed. The training officer wanted to issue a relegation certificate to him and all such officer cadets, but did not do so, given that these boys had in effect run the entire 10 km stretch twice as a punishment.

After completing his training, my father was commissioned as a Second Lieutenant in September 1963. His first posting was at Pathankot in Punjab. He had wanted a posting in the AEC, which was the Army Education Corps, but got ASC which was the Army Service Corps. My mother, supportive as always, joined him in October 1963 at Pathankot in Punjab. Initially living in a small one-bedroom flat, they were eventually allotted a spacious two-bedroom bungalow on the outskirts of Pathankot. He was posted at RHPD, the Rail Head Petroleum Depot. Here he made friends with Second Lieutenant Balgu and with Major Bahl who was his Boss.

Life was good. He had an orderly, nowadays called a buddy, who would assist him in his daily chores and help around the house too. They had a beautiful garden with colorful flowers and a kitchen garden where my mother grew fresh vegetables. The day started with morning PT (Physical Training) which was followed by office work from 8 am to 1 pm. Afternoons were restful at home

whilst evenings were usually spent with colleagues and their wives at the Games center or the Mess over a glass of Rum. My mother, although feeling somewhat out of place among the stylish and modern army wives, earned admiration and respect for her exceptional singing ability, often performing popular songs by Madan Mohan, with "*Yu Hasraton Ke Daag*" being a favorite.

And then started the 1965 Indo-Pak war.

My father and his colleagues were sitting in their Boss' cabin when they suddenly heard enemy planes hovering above. They immediately took shelter in the trenches that were made in their office compound. The sub-area Commander announced that war had been declared and all families needed to be moved out of Pathankot. Blackouts were common every other evening, which mymother experienced before she was moved to Delhi by the Army. At the start of the war, when my father was away for a few days at Hissar in Haryana, she had to live all alone in the bungalow. She had once told me how she would hear bombs dropping and at times it would be so close to their house that the windowpanes would start shattering

The enemy was targeting the RHPD and RHSD and kept bombarding it. In any war, if services are attacked and the army doesn't get its provisions including ammunition, that's the best situation for the enemy to create. My father remembers the several casualties that happened all around him and how he was

assigned the task of getting funeral arrangements done for the deceased.

He recollects a peculiar incident during the way when my mother had safely reached her maternal home in Jhansi and he was alone at Pathankot. He woke one morning to find his face covered in painful, pus-filled boils that had suddenly erupted. Perplexed by this unusual condition, which didn't resemble pimples or acne, he decided to wait a day before seeking medical attention. That afternoon, hiding his face, he went to a nearby bookshop to buy some stationary for his unit. It was a Sunday. To kill time, he started glancing through booklets containing syllabi of an MA degree from Punjab University. The booklets contained syllabi for each subject. To his utter surprise, he found that at the top of each subject syllabus, it was written that students could answer the questions in the exams in either English, Hindi, Punjabi, or Gorkhali. However, only for the syllabus of English subject, it was written that answers should be given in English only. He was truly amused. The amusement brought a smile to his face despite the soreness he had on his face which was creating a lot of pain in his jaw. There was a *panbeedi* shop just outside the bookshop. The *paanwala* had seen my father's face and asked him what happened. He said he had a remedy. He gave my father a few betel leaves and some wet *choona* and told him to go home, take the stalk of the betel leaf, and apply the *choona* on the boils with it. Fortunately, this hack worked, and the boils disappeared the next day. They had been of such a magnitude that my father was worried that they would leave scars on his face. Thankfully none of that happened and it was possibly some allergy that had been at play.

When the war was finally over, families were brought back, and my father was transferred to Udhampur in the state of Jammu and Kashmir. Udhampur was a field station. My parents lived in a Basha, a small military housing unit. My mother would cook food from the daily ration they received from the Army. He was posted as an Adjutant Transport Column which in effect was the cadre of a Captain. His immediate Boss was Major U.N. Sharma

Once, at a social outing, Major Sharma discovered my father's hidden love for theatre. This passion was latent for many years so when the Major showed interest, my father's joy knew no bounds. The Major suggested meeting the Brigadier who was keen on setting up a skit with army personnel who were keen on acting. The Brigadier's wife was producing the play, and one Colonel's wife was the Director. My father met them and was selected as the hero of this play. The heroine was the Major's wife. This Hindi play was borrowed from a book called *Saat Natak*. The Army Officers Institute was hosting this play as part of its entertainment package for all personnel.

There were 3 shows held, one for officers and two for jawans. Lt. General KP Candeth, GOC in C, 15th corps was the Chief Guest and he complimented and patted my father on his back after watching the show. This was a moment of pride and joy. The play had become an instant hit and my father got accolades and recognition for his acting prowess. View its success, it was decided to take the play all over India to all the regions and stage it at various Army installations. The first such show was to be staged in Srinagar.

That's when tragedy struck.

The heroine's husband was Major Bhargava. He was the Commanding officer of an Army transport Company. He and my father were traveling back in the Major's jeep to their Housing Unit. At the entry gate, they realized that the guards were taking too long to open the gate. My father jumped out of the jeep and went inside through the small pedestrian gate to assess why the gate was not being opened. He was shocked by the gory sight that he witnessed on the other side. Three jawans were lying dead in a pool of blood. He rushed back and reported this to the Major. It was a case of two murders and one suicide on account of some old enmity. An inquiry was initiated. This gory incident dampened the spirit of the entire unit which resulted in putting the initiative of the play going all over India on hold. Finally, that never happened.

The war ended. After winning this 1965 war, it was time for the Government to review the extra men they had hired through the Emergency Commission route. My father was one of them. He was called for an interview at Bengaluru for permanent commissioning. However, his age was just a little over the cutoff limit. The other criterion adopted by them was to release those officers who had held a good job before getting commissioned. My father sadly met both the criteria for disqualification. He was over the age limit and also had a good Government job as a lecturer earlier.

The resilient man with a positive attitude took this setback in his stride and looked ahead. He was disheartened but told himself that he was perhaps slated for greener pastures in life. He was given a warm farewell by the team. My mother sang some lovely songs at his farewell party. Thus ended a short but promising innings as Captain in the Indian army (14th April 1963 to 27th September 1967). He feels proud and fortunate to have participated in fighting for his country in the big war of 1965.

■ ■ ■

9

The loss of a Guru: his mother departs

Between 1962 to 1967, my parents faced significant challenges on the personal front. My mother experienced multiple miscarriages and was diagnosed with a weak uterus which implied the possibility of them remaining childless. At the Jallandhar military hospital, the gynecologist gave the verdict that they should try adoption as the uterus would be unable to retain a fetus beyond two months. This was truly disheartening but again my resilient parents took this setback in their stride.

At the same time, my father's mother was battling uterine cancer by 1965, which meant that he had to keep traveling back to Indore from his Army postings to see her. My grandmother could sense my father's anxiety over their inability to bear a child. Being a deeply religious person with a positive outlook, she reassured my parents that they would soon be blessed with a child.

She had also sensed that both her sons Achyut and Vasant were religion-agnostic and tending toward becoming *nastik*. Aware that after her passing, they would not be able to continue with the religious traditions and rituals that she so earnestly had practiced all her life, she did not want to push them to follow what they did not endorse full-heartedly. Hence few weeks before her death, she got everyone together and asked her two sons if they would like to continue doing all rituals after her death. Whilst neither candidly said no, she gauged their disinterest and with full acceptance asked them not to stress about it. There were several idols that she had collected and worshipped over the years. The ones made in silver were gifted to the Ganesh mandir. She instructed the sons to do a *visarjan* of the other idols in the Ganesh Mandir well. Only a picture of Chhatrapati Shivaji Maharaj praying to the goddess Bhavani was kept for inspiration in the *devghar.*

This was indeed a rare woman of her time.

On the day of her death, my grandmother had a premonition that her time had come. The customary practice during the *sutak* period after a person's death is that no food is cooked in the house for a few days. She called my aunt and my mother, who were in the house, and instructed them to quickly prepare lunch. Sensing the urgency, she asked them to call my father Achyut and his brother Vasant and insisted that all four of them should have an early lunch

Tragedy finally struck that day. It was the 20th of April 1966. In those days my father was undergoing weapons training at MHOW near Indore. He would come home to Indore every Saturday and go back on Monday morning. On April 7, 1966, a Thursday, he unexpectedly encountered his friends Narayan and Radhu at the training grounds. He sensed that they had come with bad news. He was distraught at the thought of his mother's death, so he quickly took two pegs of Gin with lime cordial, and rushed to Indore in Radhu's car. His brother-in-law Kibesaheb had organized the funeral by then. It was the saddest day of his life to lose his goddess and his guru, his mother. He was sad he was not with her when she breathed her last. Even today he fondly remembers his mother and shares several incidents which tell me how he worshipped her. He has been a *matrubhakt* in the real sense.

Let me quote a few instances here of his mother Radhabai's immense maturity and progressive thought process.

Once in a rare moment, my father, and his best friend Narayan, decided to secretly smoke a cigarette on the balcony. As luck would have it, his mother caught them in the act. Instead of firing them, she just said *"Ikde tar udbattya petlya aahet"* (incense sticks are lit here) and simply walked away. Later that night she called him beside her and explained the hazards of smoking and how he should avoid it. In a similar incident, when she realized her husband would chew tobacco and she had failed in getting him to stop it, she started cleaning the tobacco he would buy so that he consumed the better part.

In another incident when my mother had gone to Jhansi for a month and did not return on the agreed date because there was some family wedding that had come up, my father confided in his mother that he was not just missing his wife but was also upset that she had not kept her word. My grandmother gave him some golden advice. She asked him never to become a slave to his wife nor to make her his slave. Maintaining understanding and dignity of the relationship was important.

My father was extremely attached to his mother. She was a mature woman and knew that he was in a stressful job in the Army as the war was on. She also knew he was sad that he was childless. Plus, he had an angry disposition. She would therefore often avoid telling him problems if any. To cite an incident, after joining the Army, on one of his visits to Indore, he chanced upon the passbook of a *Pedhi* at his mother's bedside below her pillow. He found that there was a loan that his mother had taken. He rushed to the *Pedhi* Manager and was apprised that the house Radhaniwas had been mortgaged. One of his siblings had asked the mother to take a loan for his new project and she had done that by mortgaging the house. Since my grandmother knew that my father would never allow the home to be mortgaged nor did she want to burden him, she had kept this a secret. She knew he would not be able to pay it out of his meager salary. However, my father could not digest the idea of his mother being in debt and immediately took action to release the mortgage. He had neither cash nor savings then. Now, in their marriage, they had received some gold coins as gifts and there was also my mother's jewelry that she had received from her parents. He spoke to my mother who readily agreed with his suggestion to keep only the *mangalsutra* and give away all the jewelry and gold coins to release the mortgage of the house. My father thus freed his mother from debt. The year was 1964.

I must admit here that my parents have both been such remarkable, simple, non-materialistic souls that till recently none of us knew about this. Neither of them ever discussed it nor mentioned it to anyone. Kudos to my mother for this largeness of heart. Not many women would do this generous act and our mother's ability to handle such matters with grace and without seeking recognition reflects her deep generosity and largeness of heart.

■ ■ ■

10

A daughter is born

After my father left the Indian Army, my parents came back to Indore at the end of September 1967. He had returned home with a new positive outlook, eager to pursue a career in academia. He spent two months there and applied to the Education department. Because he had a guaranteed job as a lecturer, he quickly landed a position at the Government Arts and Commerce College in Indore, teaching Economics.

As soon as they returned to Indore, my father took my mother to see Dr. Ranga Muley, a well-known gynecologist who had recently returned from abroad with new medical knowledge. Although my mother didn't have trouble getting pregnant, she had been diagnosed with a weak uterus. Dr. Muley prescribed a 21-day course of medicine to be taken over three months. Thankfully, she conceived in December 1967. Due to her weak uterus, she was advised total bed rest throughout the pregnancy with some additional treatment to support the fetus. Dr. Muley assured my parents that if the first pregnancy went well, having another child would not be an issue.

I was born a healthy baby girl weighing eight and a half pounds at Dr. Muley's nursing home on the evening of August 3rd, 1968. My father was overjoyed, and my mother, after enduring 30 hours of labor, was ecstatic to finally become a mother after a six-year wait. My maternal grandmother Kaku, my mother's brother Yeshamama, and my father's best friend Narayan Joshi were all at the hospital to welcome me into this world. Nearly 100 people were invited to my naming ceremony, which took place at Radha Niwas. My father, known for his meticulous planning, made a detailed list of guests, the food menu, and budgeted costs for each item. The refreshments were simple—samosas, jalebis, wafers, and cold drinks. What made the invitation unique was that the invitation was from me, announcing my name. They had chosen the name Anuradha, in memory of my late grandmother Radhabai Potdar, who had passed away two years earlier.

From the printed invitation card announcing my birth in 1968 to my first job appointment letter in 1990, my father has meticulously maintained a file dedicated to me. It contains everything from my earliest handwriting and drawings to every report card and academic document. The file is impeccably organized in chronological order with an index, and my father's comments in red ink adorned all my report cards. While some teachers may have been annoyed by parental comments on report cards, that was just my father being himself—pure and unfiltered. My father was thrilled beyond measure to become a father, and I quickly became the apple of his eye. He loved seeing me dressed in cute frocks when he returned from work and would insist on changing my clothes five times a day.

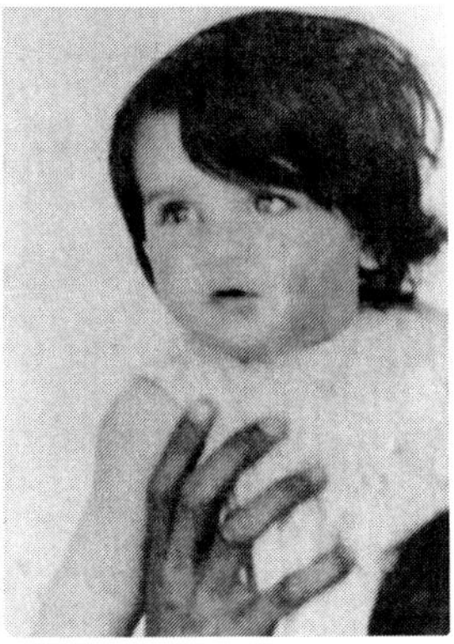

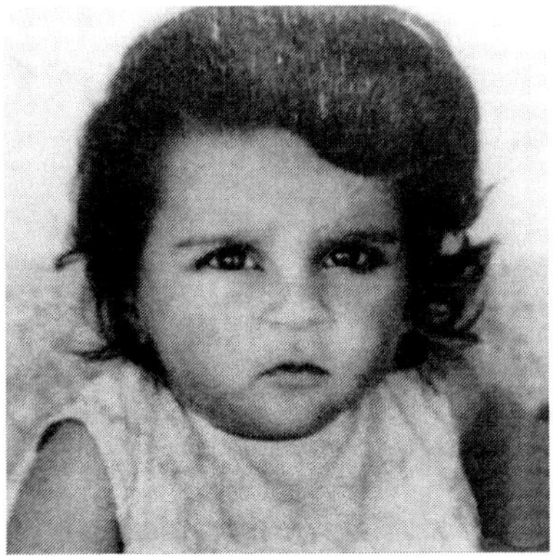

He spoiled me endlessly until my brother was born twenty months later. I've been told he used to make me sit on the floor and scatter pulses so I could pick them up one by one, keeping me occupied. He then took it upon himself to give me a haircut, whilst I kept busy trying to pick up the grains. Needless to say, those haircuts were not exactly professional, which means I did look funny in some of the pics back then!

Father's haircut

2 children followed

■ ■ ■

11

Indianoil and a life of integrity

After leaving the Army in 1967, my father's career took an unexpected turn. Just before his farewell, he and his colleague Captain M. Krishnamoorty had seen a newspaper ad for Assistant Manager positions at Indianoil Corporation Limited, with two positions reserved for Released Emergency Commission officers like themselves. They both applied immediately and were invited for interviews in Delhi in October 1967, with the Indian Army covering their travel expenses.

He narrates some incidents from that interview with Indianoil. One of the questions they asked him was about his extracurricular interests and hobbies. He replied Acting and Music. The interviewer seemed to have some knowledge of music, so he asked my father to name his favorite raga. The answer given was raga *Maalkauns*. The question then asked was what was unique about this raaga. My father correctly answered that in this raaga, the *pancham swar* is dropped. The interviewer then asked him to sing a song in this raaga.

My father said he was not a singer but was learning to play violin and could whistle. The interviewer asked him to sing the song with a whistle and my father sang *Munn tadpat hari darshan ko aaj.* The interviewer was happy. Another question asked was about his most important and secretive assignment in the Indian Army. My father replied that he had signed the Official Secrets Act and would not be able to answer this question. The interviewers were impressed with his integrity and candor. Needless to say, he got the job and so did his colleague Mr. Krishnamoorty.

Now, after returning to Indore from Udhampur in September 1967, my father had begun working as a lecturer of Economics at the Government College of Arts and Commerce. He had not heard back from Indianoil about the job he had applied for and had assumed that he had not been selected. So, he had happily settled into his new role. However, he had not heard from

Indianoil because his appointment letter had been sent to Udhampur, to his previous posting, and had been then redirected to Pathankot, before finally reaching Indore in early January 1968. By then, the joining date had passed. So on receiving it, he promptly contacted Indianoil's HR department, who agreed to set a new joining date for him: January 27th, 1968. He resigned from the College job and reported for his new job at Mumbai. After completing three months of training in Mumbai, he was assigned to the Indore office in April 1968. Unfortunately, by the end of that year, the Indore office closed down and the team was relocated to Bhopal. Thus, my father, along with my mother and me, moved to Bhopal.

They say well begun is half done. Well, Indianoil being a public sector company had people working for years together. A young ex-Army officer, intelligent and honest, joining as Assistant Manager in B grade directly was not an idea that the officers in lower grades could digest. Trouble started from day one when coteries at the office ensured that obstacles came in the way of my father's smooth sail. This marked the beginning of a challenging yet eventful journey with Indianoil for my father

To cite an example. Upon joining the Bhopal office, my father became involved in securing NOCs (No Objection Certificates) for new petrol pumps. There was an annual competition in the Western region for the district setting up the highest number of petrol pumps. Rajkot office often would win this competition with Bhopal coming second. Determined to win that year, the new boss at the Bhopal office pushed my father to clear more pump applications. However, a junior group convinced the boss that my father was selectively issuing NOCs for personal gain, causing fewer applications to be filed from the Bhopal team. In reality, my father's strict adherence to due diligence meant he was only passing applications that met all criteria. This resulted in fewer numbers submitted and, consequently, Bhopal couldn't win the award. As a punishment, my father was sent alone to Khandwa for a month without local team support. In another incident, my father rightfully claimed a first-class train fare which he was eligible for but had misplaced his ticket. The coterie convinced the Boss that he was lying and had traveled by Bus. The Boss stopped his increment for that year on the grounds of a false claim.

Thus began a journey with dismay. As he went along, he realized that his honesty and integrity were getting him punishments instead of accolades. But he was a man of high integrity and driven by sincerity and perfection. He did not lose hope.

The next posting was in Mumbai. This was from 1970 to 1972. My brother Amrish was born in 1970 whilst my mother was in Jhansi at her parental home for the delivery. That is when my father moved from Bhopal to Mumbai. We lived in Bandra in Amarjivan society on Turner Road in those days. He admitted me to Durello Convent in the nursery class. My brother was a toddler, yet too small to go to school. He was born a blue baby and was diagnosed with very early signs of polio. One day as he was playing with me, my mother noticed some

At Mumbai, 1970

weakness in one of his legs. She immediately alerted my father who rushed him to our family Doctor SG Gokhale. It was detected very early and with God's grace and the efforts of my mother, my brother got fine very quickly with no traces of polio left in his legs. It was in his Mumbai posting that he bought a second-hand, green-colored Ambassador car in which he would drive down to his Prabhadevi office from Bandra sometimes. Most of the time, he took the train or the bus. Our society was right next to actress Mala Sinha's bungalow and opposite that was Mandar nursing home, run by Dr Warty and Dr Desai where my sister, Aparna was born in 1972.

My father was transferred to Rajkot in 1973. This posting presented new challenges, especially with language. I was enrolled in Nirmala Convent, a prestigious school where Gujarati was the primary language of instruction. This posed difficulties for me, as I struggled

At Rajkot, 1974

and often came home crying. I also got lower marks due to the language barrier. My father made all efforts to make the teachers understand his child's problem by requesting them time and again to speak English in the class instead of Gujarati so that his child would understand what was going on and also learn English. He also asked the housemaid to teach me Gujarati at home. He started subscribing to a Gujarati newspaper so that both he and my mother could start reading and understanding Gujarati better and teach me.

During this time, my father also faced some personal tragedies. He lost both his older brothers unexpectedly, one in Bhopal and the other in Mumbai when he was at Rajkot. Both were in their early sixties. My father got worried if he would be the next, what with a young wife and three small children. He therefore advised my mother to go to Jhansi to her maternal home with the children and enhance her qualifications. This would help her remain independent in case anything happened to him. My mother took his advice and pursued her B. Ed in 1972 -73 as a result, supported by her family in Jhansi who lovingly cared for us during her studies. It stood her in good stead in later years when she took up teaching as a profession. Me and my brother were schooled in Jhansi at St. Francis Convent. My father would keep complete control of our progress. In those days telephones were far and few so he would write several letters and keep in touch with his family at Jhansi

In 1975, my father was transferred from Rajkot to Nagpur. We settled into a beautiful, rented bungalow in Abhyankar Nagar. The house was adjacent to open land belonging to the Vishwesaraiyya Regional Engineering College, offering a serene environment with two bedrooms, a kitchen, a spacious living room, and a dining area. It also had a servant quarter, lawns all around, a large verandah, and a terrace. I have vivid memories of the berry, mango, and moringa trees in the backyard, and the Parijat tree near our entry gate. My mother had also planted roses and moghra(jasmine) in the front garden, creating a fragrant and picturesque setting for us every morning. By

At Nagpur, 1976

this time, my brother and I were growing up. Both of us were admitted to Mount Carmel Convent School at Dhantoli and my little sister went to a local playschool nearby. Cycle rickshaws were our daily mode of transport to school.

A badminton net on our lawns, lots of nice families as neighbors, and lots of playtime with friends. We truly were a happy family enjoying life together. Before that, we had hardly lived together, and we were also too young to recollect much today. My father had sold off his Ambassador car and had now bought a second-hand Fiat MHX 7359 at Nagpur. He would drive down daily to his office at Dharampeth. When he returned home in the evenings, we eagerly awaited his arrival to open the gates into his garage—a cherished routine for us children.

He had two very good friends at Nagpur who were his colleagues in Sales, VK Sahni and Mehmood Quli Khan. They all continue to be connected even today. There was a lot of socializing with these two families when we lived in Nagpur. However, not all was smooth sailing at work. Whilst he had two good friends, he was faced with a difficult boss. Being honest and candid has its share of troubles. Bosses do not like being told if they are not right. My father never really developed tact or diplomacy and was as plain vanilla as was made naturally. The troubles started again. His assistant and his boss both were difficult and in sync, so there was double trouble brewing most of the time. There was also a luck factor that he attributes, which came in the way of his growth.

To cite a few incidents.

My father was handling Statistics and TBA sales (TBA

stood for tyres, batteries, and accessories). These were sold at petrol pumps. In 1976, the Nagpur office topped TBA sales amongst six offices in the region. Instead of getting an outstanding report for great performance, the boss commended someone else for some other achievement. Since only 25 percent of people could get an outstanding, it was a matter of choice for the Boss. My father was not given his due.

In another incident, he got caught in a very unique imbroglio. The Nagpur office was handling sales of Indane gas in Jabalpur and Damoh districts, whilst technical support was given by the Bhopal office. In his data analysis, my father discovered some fake entries and brought this to the notice of his boss. However, the officer in the Bhopal office who had facilitated these entries outsmarted him. He deceived the boss by falsely claiming credit for uncovering the frauds and misleadingly portrayed my father as taking undue credit. This manipulation not only allowed the officer to evade responsibility but also led to his promotion the following year, based on false achievements. This was a case of plain vanilla naivety and the inability of my father to advocate himself effectively.

Integrity has always been the cornerstone of my father's life. Even in his career at Indianoil, where he had opportunities to bend rules and favor acquaintances with gas connections to petrol pumps or agencies, he chose honesty and diligence My cousin Vijay Kibe tells me that he had once applied for a gas agency. My father's assistant suggested to him that he need not declare the relationship as Kibe and Potdar surnames

need not be associated. My father got angry with him for even suggesting something like that. He went ahead and declared the relationship and the application was rejected as employees' relatives were not allowed as dealers. Such was his integrity. Despite his steadfast ethics, my father often faced setbacks and slower career growth than he deserved at Indianoil. These challenges, coupled with the stress they caused, may have contributed to his development of peptic ulcers during his time in Nagpur. To manage this health issue, he started drinking *chhaas* daily, a remedy that helped control his condition for many years.

It was unfortunate that despite having the acumen

and putting in hard work with the highest level of ethos, he did not grow commensurately at Indianoil.Since there was little joy in the routine life going on at work, he indulged in theatre whilst at Nagpur as a part-time hobby. Acting was always his first passion and love. Theatre, and therefore the city of Mumbai beckoned him. In one of the visits of the Branch Manager to the Nagpur office, my father requested a transfer to Mumbai to enable him to fulfill his interest in acting.The boss agreed and May 1978 found us arriving in Mumbai, the city we have been inhabiting for the last 46 years. Indianoil would give accommodation to all its managers across the country. They either owned the accommodation or leased it. Generally, the accommodations were very good.

12

Simplicity and discipline: Family life in Mumbai

My father came to Mumbai earlier than us, to organize accommodation as well as our school admissions. We settled into a small apartment in a building called Nair Mahal in Mahim. To us, it felt cramped, resembling three railway compartments more than a traditional apartment. Coming from our spacious bungalow in Nagpur, we were initially disappointed with the living conditions, though we kept our feelings to ourselves. Nair Mahal faced water scarcity issues, with water available only from 7 am to 7.30 am daily. My father, known for his discipline, ensured we woke up early every day to finish our morning routines within this limited window. The bathroom was tiny, equipped with a large drum filled by a rubber pipe connected to the tap, which supplied our daily water needs. We also filled buckets daily for additional usage throughout the day. Early mornings were a bustling time in our household. My mother woke up early to prepare meals, meticulously packing two tiffin boxes for each of us—one for a short

break and another for lunch. My sister and I attended Canossa Convent, while my brother went to St. Michael's School, both conveniently located in Mahim. Initially, we took school buses, but as we grew older, my sister and I walked to school, and my brother took the BEST bus number 70.

In 1980, my mother took up a job as a schoolteacher on a substitute basis at King George High School Dadar. Our next-door neighbor Mrs. Nair taught there, and she helped my mother fill up a vacancy for 3 months. My mother then took up a permanent job as a Hindi teacher at Bai Avabai Framji Petit School at Pali Hill, Bandra. Our daily routine meant that we would all leave home between 8 am and 9 am daily, the earliest being my mother who took a train to Bandra and then the BEST bus no 211 to her school. The last person to leave would usually be my father who either took a train or drove down to his office.

From 1978 to 1987, our family lived in this house

in Mahim. While the house itself wasn't anything remarkable, its greatest asset was its incredibly convenient location. Perhaps that was the driving factor that had made my father accept this place. Matunga Road station was hop skip and jump away. I later joined Ruparel College in 1983 which was also just 300 meters away and I would walk it up daily to College.

Our formative years were spent within the confines of this Mahim house. Here's a glimpse into its layout: upon entering, there was a lobby leading to three equally sized rooms on the left side. The lobby ended with a shared toilet and bathroom. Each of the three rooms had a connecting door in the center. The first room on the left functioned as a living room during the day and transformed into the children's bedroom at night. It contained a small sofa set, a diwan (a type of couch), and a television on a table. My brother slept on the diwan, while my sister and I shared a mattress on the floor. The middle room featured a wooden partition that separated the kitchen from the dining area. This dining room was where my father had wooden shelves installed on the walls to store our books. There was a dining table with 6 chairs and a big fridge kept in this small dining room as a result of which there was little space left to move around. The third room was our parents' bedroom with a spacious double bed and two Godrej almirahs in which we kept all our clothes. The long lobby from the entry door to the toilet bathroom area had shoe shelves and some storage spaces.

My father was exceptionally strict—a true disciplinarian. Education and studies were his unwavering focus. As the clock approached 6 pm, his usual arrival time from the office, my siblings and I hurriedly tidied any mess, opened our books, and seated ourselves at the dining table. Often, we pretended to study.6 pm to 9 pm was study time and we were not allowed to talk a word with each other despite all three of us sitting at the same table. We were children so there was a naughty streak in each one of us. We wanted to talk, and pin-drop silence was frustrating. Sometimes we would write on chits and pass on the chits to each other to escape his watchful eye. But as luck would have it, he was too smart for us. He would check the small compartments below the table to find our crushed chits there and then fire us. In the bedroom, there was a large single-seater sofa chair where he'd sit in the evenings with his glass of rum, strategically positioned to keep an eye on us at the dining table. He would get up often and come to check what we were studying. Often, he would find that the page of our textbook was the same for very long. The firing was followed by a spanking at times! I recall a time when my brother, caught off guard by the doorbell, quickly flipped his book upside down—something that didn't escape our father's notice, leading to undesirable consequences.

Despite his involvement in theatre and professional pursuits, his attention to us children was impeccable. He closely monitored our school progress, adding his comments to our report cards that occasionally embarrassed us before our teachers. If any of us faltered in a subject, we could expect swift discipline. We held him in both fear and reverence, knowing that his high standards were non-negotiable. In our household, he was the unequivocal authority figure, and my mother and siblings alike adhered to his expectations without question.

We had several guests coming and staying with us in that small house. Our study schedules were not allowed to change. My father and his younger brother who often came and stayed with us for long durations, would have visitors who were interesting folks. They would sit and have *gupshup* and often there were music sessions too in the living room. They would close the connecting door so that we could keep studying in the middle room. But as expected, our ears would be outside. I remember hearing the famous music Director C Ramchandra singing in the living room. Music Director Sajjad Hussain would also come over sometimes with my uncle. Nana Patekar who lived two buildings away in those days and was a young actor in Marathi theatre, would also drop by to have a cup of tea. Govind Nihalani, Om Puri, and Amrish Puri were some others I remember seeing as a child in our house.

Television viewing was a regulated privilege, contingent upon our daily study habits and academic performance. My father meticulously determined what and how much we could watch. We eagerly awaited programs like *Chitrahaar,* Marathi movies on Saturdays, Hindi movies on Sundays, and other favorites such as *Saptahiki, Humlog, Buniyaad, Ramayan, Mahabharat, and Rajni.*Radio played a significant role in our daily routine. Mornings from 6.30 am to 8 am and evenings from 9 pm to 11 pm were designated radio times. My parents particularly enjoyed listening to ghazals by Ghulam Ali, whose cassettes filled our home and we still know the lyrics by heart.

Enrolling us in children's theatre was another initiative my father took. We became part of a children's theatre called *Chandrashala*, an initiative of the *Avishkaar* theatre group founded by Sulbha and Arvind Deshpande. Children from various schools like King George, Balmohan Vidyamandir, Saraswati Vidyalaya, and a few other schools participated in it. We had a total of around 75 children in the group and those were fun times for us. We did 3 dance dramas with a duration of almost three hours. *Apna Haath Jagannath, Panchatantra, and Durga Zali Gauri* were the titles. Popular actress Urmila Matondkar was also a part of this group. Music for all three musical dance dramas was composed by a duo called Shank Neel, two young and bright music directors. We remember the songs to date and sometimes reminisce about those days dancing to those steps. They were indeed so melodious and hummable. Every Sunday, the great dance master Guru Parvathikumar and his disciple, the famous dance teacher Sandhya Purecha would teach us Bharat Natyam to enable graceful movements in the dance dramas. We did multiple roles and it used to be fun changing clothes to play different characters and doing makeup for the same.

This extracurricular activity continued from 1979 to 1982. By 1983, when I reached class ten, our participation came to an end. It was a phase we truly cherished. Together, we performed approximately 100 shows featuring all three titles. Our troupe traveled to Indore for 5 shows and to Shri Baba Amte's Anandvan at Warora near Nagpur for 7 shows. Throughout these journeys, my father and mother accompanied us to every outstation performance, showing steadfast support for our endeavors.

My father was strict no doubt but there was also that softer side of him that we would experience now and again. We eagerly awaited those nights when he would be in a good mood and take us for ice cream in Juhu. In our aqua-green Fiat car, we would drive from Mahim to Juhu Beach to enjoy Vadilal ice cream. These outings happened perhaps once every two months and were truly joyful occasions for us. Indian Oil granted him a leave travel concession once every two years. The company owned beautiful holiday homes in nearly all hill stations across India. Our first family vacation was to Coonoor near Ooty in 1981. We traveled by first-class train up to Bangalore and then continued to Mysore and Ooty

In 1983, we visited Kashmir. By then, my father was eligible for flight fares, so we flew to Delhi and Jammu, then journeyed by road from Jammu to Srinagar through the scenic Nehru tunnel. My father ensured our family experienced everything Kashmir had to offer. Having spent considerable time in the region during his Army days, he took us to enjoy paneer *pakodas* at *dhabas* along the highways, ride horses, boat in shikaras on Dal Lake, and pose for photographs in Kashmiri attire. Our stay at the holiday home was delightful, and we were accompanied by the Kasbekar family, close friends of my parents.

My father was a completely religion-agnostic, anti-rituals man. My mother, while not very religious herself, had significantly reduced whatever rituals she had earlier practiced, after her marriage. However, during their time in the Army, after experiencing a few miscarriages, she had once visited the Vaishnodevi temple with some other Army wives. At that time, she had secretly made a *mannat* (a vow) to have a child. She promised that if she were blessed with a child, she would bring the child to the temple for a *darshan* (divine viewing). She chose not to tell my father about this vow then. The Kashmir holiday presented a golden opportunity for her to fulfill her *mannat.* Surprisingly, my father agreed to let her fulfill her commitment and took us to Katra village, the starting point for the climb to the Vaishnodevi temple. True to his principles, he did not accompany us on the climb, opting instead to wait at the foothills in a *dhaba*

We began our climb at 7 am, reaching the temple around 1 pm after walking nearly 14 km through undulating and rough terrain with cold November winds blowing. The entire journey was marked by chants of *"Jai Mata Di"* from people going up and coming down, which my mother said gave us the energy to keep going. In those days, the roads were not well-developed, making the journey quite tedious. At the temple, my mother wanted to present me, the *mannat* child, before the Goddess. But the crowd was rough and unruly and I remember getting pushed away even before I could get the *darshan* properly. When we came back down, my father narrated an amusing incident from his time waiting at the dhaba. While he was sitting and having some beer, a beggar approached him, saying, "*Sahab, darshan kijiye, yaha sabki dua poori hoti hai*". My father, with his characteristic wit, asked the beggar, "*Aapne kiya kya*?"The beggar replied, "*Hum to roz karte hai*". My father asked him "*Fir aapki poori kyu nahi hui*?". The beggar, offended, angrily walked away.

1985. I had taken my 12th standard examinations and secured 96% in Physics Chemistry and Biology which made me eligible to get a seat in the best medical colleges in Mumbai. However, I did not want to pursue a career in medicine as my passion lay in engineering. Unfortunately, I did not achieve the full marks I had anticipated in Mathematics due to a major cheating incident at my exam center, which resulted in negative marks for all students. Despite a signature campaign to protest the unfair penalization, our efforts were in vain. As a result, I did not secure admission to top engineering colleges like VJTI or SP. My father was staunchly against the capitation fees demanded by private colleges such as Thadomal Shahani in those days. Since I was good at drawing and art, at the insistence of a friend I took the entrance exam for Architecture. I got selected and started my Architecture course at Rachana Sansad's Academy of Architecture at Prabhadevi. The point to be noted here is that while my father was very particular about our education, he never influenced, demanded, or pushed any specific profession on us. He always assured us that he would support whatever career paths we chose.

In November 1985 my father had taken us for a holiday to Darjeeling. We flew to Kolkata and Bagdogra and then hired a taxi to Darjeeling. This was a memorable trip as my aunt Lila Maushi, her husband Dr. Tikekar, and their son Nikhil accompanied us. I have vivid memories of this trip. One chilly morning, all of us got wrapped in warm clothes from head to toe leaving noses exposed. We went to see Mt. Kanchenjunga from a point called Tiger Hill. As we shivered in the cold, waiting for the sunrise to cast its first rays on the peak, we heard a lot of noise. My father quickly fronted us and pushed us behind some trees. We saw a mob chasing a man without clothes, wielding sticks. They all quickly disappeared downhill. Later, my father told us that there was a high chance that the mob would have killed that man. Even now, the memory of what that poor man endured in the biting cold of minus 4 degrees sends shivers down my spine.

My father had a habit of drinking two pegs of rum daily since his Army days. In those early years in Mumbai, he also smoked a cigarette or two with his drinks. During that Darjeeling trip, one evening, he was smoking and suddenly called the three of us to try a puff. My mother was shocked and a bit angry. He explained that he didn't want us, now teenagers, to be curious and secretly try smoking. He wanted us to experience it openly, in his presence. This approach seemed to work because, from that day until today, none of us were ever drawn to smoking. He applied the same logic to alcohol, allowing us to taste it with him. It was a very progressive approach for those times.

The most life-changing experience was yet to happen in Darjeeling. I had finished one semester of Architecture and realized that I was just not liking it. I felt I was not in the right career and had made a big mistake. I was very scared of my father's reaction and thought he would be really angry. However, I knew I had to address the issue. I knew I had to bell the cat. During this holiday, while feeling stressed and unable to truly enjoy myself, I mustered all my courage, took a piece of paper, and wrote a letter to my father. I explained that I was not suited for architecture and wanted to exit the course, pursue a B. Sc, and eventually write my MBA. One night, I placed the letter near his pillow. The following night, I found the same paper near my pillow. In his reply, my father wrote that I should go ahead and do what felt right for me and assured me that I would always have his support.

On returning to Mumbai, we rushed to Ruparel College and met the Principal, Dr. A. P. Pradhan. He told my father that he could give me admission on the condition that I would have to score a minimum of 70 marks out of 100 on all six papers. These marks would then be averaged, with the cutoff to pass being 35. This was necessary because I had missed one full semester. My father agreed and assured the Principal that his daughter would study hard and achieve over 70 marks. Thankfully, I met the challenge and stood first in all streams of B. Sc in both my first and second years. My proudest moment was when my father attended the award ceremony where I received the prize. The year was 1987.

The 1987 holiday to Goa was perhaps the last big family holiday we had, as afterward, we all became busy with our post-graduation studies and careers. This was also the year we moved home from Mahim to Pali Hill, Bandra. This was a dramatic change that made all of us very happy. My father had finally been allotted a better accommodation. This was after he seriously took our persuasion in the years before and applied for a change. Left to him, he would never aspire to change the status quo. The new house was a lovely and spacious two-bedroom apartment on the first floor of a building called Bajaj Jade. My mother's school was just a stone's throw away, and the neighborhood was posh and stylish. We made new friends in the building, and the entire area was home to film stars and other celebrities. It was overall a very peaceful place to live, just near the Carter Road seaside. Walks along Carter Road were a delight, and both my brother and I learned to drive while we lived in that house. I started working at Godrej Soaps in May 1990 after completing my MBA and got a Maruti 800 car from the office. Driving it with music along Carter Road on weekends became a joyful habit. I got married in the Pali Hill home in July 1992 in a registered marriage as my father did not believe in the Vedic rituals of marriage and wanted to keep it simple. He threw a reception for around 200 people in a nice hotel in Juhu the next day.

My father retired in October 1992, but we were allowed to keep the office accommodation until April 1993. By this time, my father had bought his own house in Bandra Reclamation. A simple man with meager savings, he exhausted all his resources to buy a modest and small two-bedroom flat in a building called Meera Madhura at Bandra Reclamation. The new house was on the 4th floor of a building constructed by middle-level ex-government officials. It had no lift, so climbing four floors daily became part of the routine, which was the reason my father got it at a lower price. This flat overlooked the Mahim Creek and later, after the Bandra-

Worli Sea Link was built, it offered a beautiful view of the same. Lilavati Hospital was just a few buildings away, making it a convenient location. My daughter was born in 1993, just as my parents moved into this new house.

As the years went by, climbing four floors daily became increasingly difficult, especially as the family expanded after my brother's marriage. With his wife and two sons added to the family, the need for more space became apparent. In 2007, my father bought two new flats in two neighboring buildings in a society in Kandivali East, Mumbai North. One flat was for him and my mother, and the other was for my brother's family. He provided my brother with a loan at no interest, which my brother systematically repaid. The idea was to allow my brother to own his home and feel pride in it, rather than receiving it for free from his parents. This was another example of my father's progressive and unique thought process.

My father has been so simple that he never had great aspirations. He has always had *samadhaan* in minimalistic living. He never made any big investments to grow his wealth. Throughout his life, he was conservative and kept his savings only in fixed deposits at his bank. Several years earlier he had invested in a small apartment in Indore, his hometown, but sold that off when he had to buy the Mumbai house in 1993. He had also bought a very small tenement in a building in Jogeshwari as part of the Army quota, which he gave away on a small rent to one of my cousins for several years before selling it at a meager price.

■ ■ ■

13

A character, unwavering

By the time he retired in October 1992, my father had served in various roles across different departments at both the Regional office as well as the Head office of Indianoil in Mumbai. Throughout his tenure, he looked after LPG sales, Personnel & Administration, and finally oversaw Public Relations. Given his flair for both oral and written communication, it was not surprising that he became the editor of the in-house magazine of the Western region, Indoil West. This posting in Mumbai allowed him to indulge in his passion for acting. However, from a professional growth perspective, it was far from fulfilling. He faced similar issues as he had in Nagpur. For instance, while working as Manager (Administration) in

the Regional Office, he discovered some staff employees cheating Indian Oil on medical claims. Instead of being appreciated for his vigilance, the uproar created by such acts often worked against him, slowing down his professional growth. However, that did not deter the workaholic in him. In one notable incident, he approached his department head and mentioned that he had some free time after completing his routine work and offered to take on additional tasks. He was promptly assigned pending work from another department, much to his immediate boss's dismay.

There was however the creative side of him that was much appreciated.

One day, the Branch Manager of Western Region, Mr. DN Sharma, called him to his cabin. He said "*You are doing such good work in films and serials, so why don't you create something with our staff members for 1st May Maharashtra Day?*" The function was to be held at the office auditorium on the 30th of April evening at 4 pm because the 1st of May was a bank holiday. My father had just a week to create a full-fledged event for this function. He conducted auditions of staff members for a skit, got one of Sai Paranjpe's skits translated from Marathi to Hindi, and shortlisted the cast. He also selected a few singers to perform after the skit. When the day arrived, he hosted the event with his classic witty style. The audience loved his wordplay and impromptu compering.

This was the beginning of a long innings of hosting several Indian Oil programs and events. In another event, he hosted the farewell function for the Regional Manager, Mr. R. M. Basrur. Displaying his characteristic wit, he creatively played with Mr. Basrur's initials, saying, "We are here to bid farewell to Regional Manager Basrur and wish that R. M. Basrur becomes G. M. Basrur, then D. M. Basrur, and finally C. M. Basrur." Here, G. M. stood for General Manager, D. M. for Director (Marketing), and C. M. for Chairman. This clever wordplay delighted the audience and solidified his reputation as a charismatic host. From that point onward, for most programs, he was the host even after his retirement. His Chairman Mr. BK Bakshi loved him. I remember in 2013 when we visited Bangalore, we visited Mr. Bakshi and received a very warm welcome at his home.

Despite the love and popularity, he enjoyed at the office, and his personality, which was marked by enthusiasm, positivity, integrity, acumen, and efficiency, his professional growth at Indianoil was not commensurate with his capabilities. When I once asked him about his career aspirations, he expressed that, had luck been on his side, he could have risen to the level of Executive Director at IndianOil. I couldn't agree more with his assessment. His career highlights the role of luck and timing in professional advancement, regardless of talent and dedication.

■ ■ ■

14

Theatre, his first love

It all started in 1946 in Indore. The Marathi drama centenary was celebrated at a place called Nandlalpura Theatre. My father's elder sister, Ambika, was married to Shri Prabhakar Kibe, a local theatre enthusiast. My father would watch all the plays in which Kibesaheb acted, and one of these plays even featured the renowned Acharya Atre. The acting bug bit him at the age of ten. My father mobilized his friends in Martand Chowk to create a play. Their first performance was a small skit from their textbook called *Ramshastri Prabhune*, staged on the terrace of his friend Narayan Joshi's house.

with Prabhakar Kibe

The audience consisted of a handful of neighborhood friends and their parents.

The following year, my father's friend Sakhya Matkar started a new group called Baal Utkarsh Mandal, aimed at encouraging and promoting theatre among children. Under this banner, my father and his friends created their first full-length play, *Simhagadh*, in which he played the role of Udaybhanu. His friend, the famous singer Arun Date, played the role of Tanaji Malusare. This play was staged on the terraces of four houses in Martand Chowk and then at ten other locations the following year. The success and confidence gained by these boys after staging *Simhagadh*, led them to create new plays for *Ganeshotsav* every year thereafter. The plays were staged at several Ganesh Mandal locations during the ten-day festival. These included the mandals at Rambaug, Krishnapura, Nathmandir, Jail Road,

The play Zunzharao

Zamindarwada, Yeshwant Road, etc. The group charged the Ganesh Mandal a fee of Rs. ten plus Tonga fare. This fee would just about cover the cost of production. They would also do extra shows for Mandals if requested and tickets would be sold at two annas per head.

His passion for acting began in school but slowed down during college. It was reignited in 1966 during his Army days when his unit staged a play called *Saat Natak*, with him in the lead role. There was another hiatus after that. In 1970, during his first job in Mumbai with Indianoil, my father had the chance to pursue acting once again. At age 36, he was in great shape and looked good, making him seem well-suited for a successful acting career. Although he started well in Mumbai's theatre scene in 1970, luck wasn't on his side once again. Indianoil regularly transferred its managers every few years, so he was moved to Rajkot in 1972 and then to Nagpur in 1975.

I sometimes wonder if he had quit his job in 1972 to focus on acting full-time, would he have achieved greater success? But perhaps it wasn't meant to be. He faced personal and professional challenges one after another. I don't know if it was the sudden loss of his two older brothers that made him feel uncertain, if he hesitated to take risks in the unpredictable film industry, if his top priority was his family responsibilities, or if he simply had an attitude of accepting life as it unfolded. He chose not to leave his job in 1972 to pursue a career in theatre and film. He believed in duty and sincerity, always putting his family first and avoiding unnecessary risks that would destabilize their security.

Looking back, none of us have any regrets because the results have been wonderful. He has successfully managed his life and family, and he has earned recognition and a place for himself in the public eye purely based on his abilities. Not many people can claim to have excelled in four different careers with equal dedication and skill in one lifetime: academics, military service, management, and acting. He is a truly versatile man.

■ ■ ■

15

His third Guru: Pandit Satyadev Dubey

During his time in Mumbai with Indianoil, from 1970 to 1972, my father became friends with a colleague named Chandrashekhar Kamerkar, who was Marathi actress Sulbha Deshpande's brother. Bapu as he was fondly known had introduced my father to Sulbha and Arvind Deshpande, a couple prominent in Mumbai's Marathi theatre scene. It was through Bapu Kamerkar that my father met his life's third Guru, Pandit Satyadev Dubey. Dubeyji was an iconic person in the Hindi theatre world and was hugely respected.

One day Bapu walked into my father's office cabin casually and they got talking. When he heard of my father's passion for acting, he asked him if he would like to join a theatre group. My father jumped at the opportunity and the group he got introduced to was called *Theatre Unit*. This group was founded by Pandit Satyadev Dubey. That very evening, after Bapu had suggested, my father went to Tardeo where rehearsals of the Hindi play *Pagla Ghoda* were on. There, he met

Dubeyji who immediately welcomed him into the group. This marked the beginning of my father's journey with Theatre Unit in Mumbai, a journey whose first phase lasted from 1970 to 1972.

In early 1973, my father was transferred to Rajkot. This move was a significant emotional and professional setback for him because he had just started to establish himself in the theatre group. *Pagla Ghoda* had been a successful play he had acted in, and he had received rave reviews in the press for the same. Unfortunately, just as he was gaining recognition as an actor, the transfer came and disrupted his momentum.

Training under Dubeyji was rigorous from the start. Being his disciple meant spending every evening observing rehearsals of ongoing plays. Rehearsals took place at venues like Chhabildas High School in Dadar or at Walchand Terraces in Tardeo, Mumbai. After finishing his office hours, my father would head straight to these locations, where he would sit and watch Dubeyji directing his actors. My father held Dubeyji in high regard and was willing to do anything for him. The practice of revering a Guru had been instilled in him since childhood by his father. He had shown deep devotion to his earlier two Gurus, his mother, and his Pol master. Now, he was ready to extend the same

Pt. Satyadev Dubey

devotion to his third Guru.

He recalls a few incidents during this time. Once, when accompanying Dubeyji to Delhi for a play they were staging, there was a function organized by the Dance Drama Academy to honor Dubeyji at 6 pm. Around 5:45 pm, while my father was in the washroom of the auditorium, Dubeyji hurriedly entered and asked my father to lend him his kurta. Dubeyji was staying at Sai Paranjpe's house in Delhi during this trip, and the laundry had not returned his clothes in time. Without hesitation, my father gave Dubeyji the kurta he was wearing, and in exchange, he wore Dubeyji's kurta, which was soaked in sweat. My father didn't mind at all, knowing it belonged to his Guru. Another example of Guru worship was when he proactively took the responsibility to clean Dubeyji's home. He had seen on a television program called "*Pratibha aani Pratima*" how many respected individuals went to great lengths to serve their Gurus, which he says, had deeply inspired him.

Now, Dubeyji was a bachelor living in a society called Sahitya Sahwas in Bandra East in Mumbai. A lot of people would visit his home and it used to always be in disarray. No one bothered to keep the teacups in the kitchen, let alone clean them. The house would be dishevcled as a result and Dubeyji was too busy to bother about it. He did not have a maid or servant in those days. My father noticed this during his visits and took it upon himself to keep Dubeyji's house in order. There was a second set of keys that Dubeyji would keep at a neighbor's place. Every Sunday at 10 am, my father would take the keys, open the house, and tidy it up. Dubeyji would either be traveling or at someone's place the previous night. My father would do the dusting, wash all utensils lying around, and tidy up the kitchen, bedroom, and living room sincerely and leave. Needless to say, my father's level of perfection transformed Dubeyji's house every Sunday. He did this *sewa* relentlessly for a long time. Since Dubeyji was used to the mess at his home, he would often look at the neat house and then at my father in an amused and baffled manner.

Dubeyji was a very strict man. He would train his group members with an acute sense of detail. Once my father was rehearsing for the play *Pagla Ghoda* at Walchand Terraces, Tardeo. Amol Palekar was an Assistant Director to Dubeyji for this play. Suddenly my father noticed a familiar face in the auditorium. It was his idol *Pu La* Deshpande who had dropped by. My father exchanged a hello with him and within a few seconds, hell broke loose. Dubeyji stopped the rehearsal and questioned my father why had he broken the character to greet *Pu La*, pointing out that the character he portrayed wouldn't have known *Pu La*. Dubeyji's strict discipline led to my father being dismissed from rehearsals for four days as punishment. This incident occurred in 1972.

During those days, Amol Palekar had not yet made his film debut. My father lived in Bandra and would drive his green Ambassador to his office at Prabhadevi before heading to Tejpal Auditorium at Tardeo for rehearsals. After rehearsals, Amol often asked my father for a ride to his fiancée Chitra Murdeshwar's residence in Colaba. After dropping Amol off, my father would return home

Pagla Ghoda

Dr. Huddar

to Bandra. During those days in the Theatre Unit, Amrish Puri was another prominent actor involved in several plays. An article in Maharashtra Times about the play "*Pagla Ghoda*" referred to "AP, AP, and AP," which stood for Amol Palekar, Amrish Puri, and Achyut Potdar.

My father also participated in a few plays with the Avishkar theatre group, which was led by Sulbha and Arvind Deshpande. However, this period of success was short-lived. "*Pagla Ghoda*" was a hit, and he was gaining recognition. His career seemed to be on the rise, but luck wasn't on his side.

In 1973, Indianoil transferred him to Rajkot, where there were no opportunities for his passion for acting. His next chance came when he was transferred to Nagpur in 1975.In Nagpur, his office was in Dharampeth. He would finish work by 6 pm, and in the evenings, he either socialized with his friends Mahmood Quli Khan or Vijay Sahni or stayed home overseeing our studies.

Jayketu

Additionally, he traveled extensively in and around Nagpur for his sales responsibilities.

In Nagpur, my father met Manohar Mhaisalkar, the head of Vidarbha Sahitya Sangha, and they became close friends. Through Manohar, he connected with local theatre enthusiasts, including producer-director duo Vishram Ansinghkar and Mahesh Paturkar. Recognizing his passion and talent, they invited my father to collaborate on three plays. One of these plays, titled "Jayketu," earned my father the Best Actor award from the Government of Maharashtra. In the three years at Nagpur, my father had kept himself busy with his passion for acting and that had got him a lot of recognition and respect in Nagpur

When he was transferred to Mumbai in 1978, his joy knew no bounds. He was finally coming back to the Mecca of theatre once again. On arrival, he reconnected with Pandit Satyadev Dubey, his guru, and rejoined the group Theatre unit. He immersed himself in numerous plays, many of which were staged at Prithvi Theatre in Juhu, Mumbai.

Once Padmashri Vijaya Mehta, the famous Marathi Director approached my father regarding a role that she had in mind for him. Now Vijayabai was a contemporary to Dubeyji professionally so out of respect for his guru, he refused the offer. Around the same time, a good friend of Dubeyji, Govind Nihalani was making the film *Aakrosh* and he had cast my father in it. One day on the sets of *Aakrosh*, Govindji advised my father to take up the role in Vijayabai's play as it would do him a lot of good. He assured my father that Dubeyji was okay with the idea. He told him that it would be foolish to not play a role in Vijayabai's play. My father was overjoyed at this assurance and was delighted to grab the opportunity of working with another great Director from the theatre

Wada Chirebandi

world. He connected with Vijayabai again and asked her if the role was still open. She had not yet found another person as apt as my father for that role.

The year was 1985. The title of the play was *Wada Chirebandi*. Written by Mahesh Elkunchwar, the play was a big success. Over fifty shows were held all over Maharashtra including Mumbai, Pune, Kolhapur, Nagpur, and Aurangabad with several shows outside Maharashtra too, in Delhi, Kolkata, and Indore. The play won the first prize in the State Government competition for commercial plays. The second prize went to the play *Natasamrat* starring Dr Sriram Lagu and the third prize went to the play *Purush* starring Nana Patekar. The competition was called the Marathi Vyavsayik Natak Spardha. It was the first year that this new award for professional theatre was created by the Government of Maharashtra. *Wada Chirebandi* got several awards including the Best Actor award, which my father proudly received. He cherishes this experience as one of life's treasures, having made his mark in a competitive field.

Later a film based on the same play was made and my father acted in it, much against Dubeyji's wishes this time. For some reason best known to him, Dubeyji did not appreciate this and severed ties with my father ever since. It was a big setback for my father when the relationship with his Guru ended like this. He was deeply hurt but he took it in his stride given that it was his Guru's decision.

The theatre journey In Mumbai was brief but am proud to say that he achieved excellence in whatever he did. He collaborated with Sulbha Deshpande and

Arvind Deshpande's group Awishkaar and got a state government award for one of their plays. The name of that play was *Mahabhojan Terawyache.*

Whilst all the plays had been going on, Sulbha Deshpande had already gotten him an entry into Hindi films no sooner than he arrived in Mumbai in 1978. Managing his Indianoil job along with the daily rehearsals for theatre was not easy. The theatre was physically very demanding and managing his office work and outstation tours was not allowing him to immerse himself fully in theatre. He thus bid goodbye to the theatre world in 1986 and continued indulging in his acting passion through films and television.

My father has acted in over 25 theatrical plays. The list of plays is appended at the end of this book

■ ■ ■

16

Into the world of Bollywood

The year was 1978.

My father began spending a lot of time with Arvind and Sulabha Deshpande, who lived just about two hundred meters away from our home in Mahim, Mumbai. They engaged in play readings, discussions, and meetings with various actors from the Marathi theatre world. It was through Sulabhatai that my father got his first break in Hindi cinema with the film "*Ramnagri*," written by Ram Nagarkar. The lead roles were played by Amol Palekar and Suhasini Mulay, and Sulabhatai herself had a significant role. Around the same time, she also recommended him for an advertisement film, marking the beginning of his journey into the world of Hindi films, television, and advertising.

His breakthrough came with a pivotal role in Govind Nihalani's "*Aakrosh*" in 1980, starring Smita Patil, Naseeruddin Shah, and Om Puri. The film garnered numerous awards, including a National Award for Best Film, six Filmfare Awards for Best Director, Actor, and

Screenplay, among others, and the Golden Peacock Best Film award at the International Film Festival of India. My father portrayed a forest contractor in this intense and critically acclaimed film. This success led to several more collaborations with Govindji.

In 1983, he acted in "*Ardhasatya,*" another award-winning film directed by Govind Nihalani, playing the role of a corrupt police officer named Inspector Patil. He continued to feature prominently in Govindji's subsequent films like "*Party,*" "*Drohkaal,*" and others, solidifying his place in Govindji's repertoire.

I recall that during the early days of "*Aakrosh,*" Govindji visited our residence in Mahim a couple of times. He was always soft-spoken, and his simplicity then, as now, is truly endearing. He even attended my wedding in 1992 and my parents' 50th wedding anniversary in 2012, demonstrating his enduring connection with our family. Another remarkable individual who became a close friend of my father was Om Puri. Omji frequently attended our significant family events, and I remember him visiting our home in Mahim on occasions to share a drink with my father. Alongside Om Puri, my father also mingled with Naseeruddin Shah and Amrish Puri during those days.

His involvement in numerous award-winning classics brought him considerable attention, catching the eye of other film directors who began casting him in their projects. Saeed Mirza featured my father in his films "*Albert Pinto Ko Gussa Kyun Aata Hai*" and "*Mohan Joshi Hazir Ho,*" making him a regular presence in his movies. Vidhu Vinod Chopra was another director who admired my father and consistently crafted roles for him in his films, continuing this collaboration up to the film "*Three Idiots*".

Now whilst the roles had started pouring in, it was not easy for my father, who worked full time in a public sector company Indianoil to do them all. Transfers were inevitable, enemies were bound to be created at work and the journey was surely not going to be smooth if he pursued two careers with equal passion. Family obligations prevented him from quitting his job. He quietly resolved not to chase ambitious goals or take significant risks. Ensuring job security was paramount to providing the best for his family. Moreover, he realized that his personality and temperament didn't align perfectly with the film industry's culture of flamboyance, networking, and socializing – these were just not aspects of his DNA.

He has been a man with strong ethics and a reserved nature, believing in earning opportunities through his performance and merit. He never promoted himself or sought roles actively. So whilst roles started coming in with higher momentum, he realized that it was important to align his Management at Indian Oil and seek official permission to act in films and television. A senior colleague suggested that he should get approval either from the Director (Marketing) or the Chairman of Indianoil. My father was in a dilemma, as his request could be refused which meant he would comply, thereby implying a full stop to acting in films. At the same time, not taking permission would have landed him in hot water anyway. He chose to take permission. He wrote a letter to the Director (Marketing), Mr. M.S. Rana through his immediate Boss Mr. A. K. Bhatnagar who was the Public Relations Manager at that time. The letter sought permission to act in films and television serials in a manner and quantum that would not affect his work and duties at Indianoil. Mr. Rana permitted him. His joy knew no bounds.

However, given that there were built-in restrictions in this permission, my father could not devote himself full-time to his acting career. He therefore chose to do *cameos* as those could be done quickly over a day or two, especially on weekends. He did not have to take any leave from his office for the same. The film industry is very smart and knows that if a person is a full-time employee in any organization, he or she cannot do justice to major roles. Therefore, cameos and small yet significant roles came his way. My father was also happy as he could now give attention to his work as well as indulge in acting as a hobby. His sincerity and commitment to his job were such that he declined a few major roles that demanded long durations of shooting. He also rejected roles that required shooting to be done outside of Mumbai.

My father narrates several interesting incidents in his film career.

Reminiscing about the two-week stay at Alibaug near Mumbai for the shooting of *Aakrosh,* his first major film in 1985, he tells me about the camaraderie among the cast and crew. Each actor was deeply committed to the film, striving to deliver their best performances. After wrapping up for the day, my father often enjoyed evening drinks with Amrish Puri and Arvind Deshpande. Smita Patil, Om Puri, and Naseeruddin Shah were remarkable co-stars, and the sets were filled with intellectual discussions. Dinner would include tasty fish preparations made from the fresh catch from the Alibaug seas. He remembers how Smita Patil would eat only the upper layer of roti with milk. That was what best suited her digestive system. She would spend a lot of time reading in between her shots. Govindji was an extremely calm and composed Director. His attention to detail was phenomenal. Once on the sets of his second film *Ardhasatya,* Govindji was about to action the shoot on a set designed as a police station. Suddenly he asked for everything to be stopped. He then asked some workers on the set to go rub their soiled hands on the walls here and there, to give it a realistic look instead of a freshly painted set. Such was his eye for detail. It was during the making of these two films that Om Puri became a good friend of my father. He truly loved and respected

Aakrosh

ArdhSatya

my father who was several years older than him and my father reciprocated it with similar love and admiration.

Once on the sets of Saeed Mirza's *Albert Pinto Ko Gussa Kyu Aata Hai*, my father had a long scene to deliver. It was a monologue, a speech addressed to the labor force. For some reason, the shoot which was to happen around noon got delayed up to six pm. Finally, when it was shot, my father delivered the scene in just one take. Being a theatre person with amazing memory and control over his dialogue delivery, it was rather simple for him to do this. The Unit was amazed, and everyone complimented him. He was often labeled as a one-take actor on most of his sets. He attributes this to the training he received from his guru Pandit Satyadev Dubey.

One day my father got a call from a man called Ramgopal Varma who requested him to meet him at his Juhu residence. My father went there and met this ordinary-looking simple young man who narrated the storyline of his film *Rangeela* to him. He asked him if he would act as the heroine Urmila Matondkar's father. My father said of course he would love to do that. There were several interesting scenes he did with Aamir Khan in this movie. He got popularity and recognition for his playful character in this film. His style of calling out to Aamir as *Munna* was loved by audiences. His scenes with Aamir where he tells him about his youth days and girlfriends became very popular. This film had some amazing music by A. R. Rehman and the film worked wonders for every single actor in the film. He developed a good rapport with Aamir Khan with whom he did a

Rangeela

few more films later. However, something went amiss between Ramgopal Varma and my father because of some misunderstanding. There was an adverse statement made in the media against Mr. Varma, which was attributed to Aamir Khan. There was a lot of controversy about it. Sadly, Mr. Varma assumed that my father had also supported that statement as he was a friend of Aamir Khan. There was cold silence after that.

The Yash Chopra film *Yeh Dillagi* with Kajol, Akshay Kumar, and Saif Ali Khan was a film where he played Kajol's father. He remembers Kajol as a vivacious person but more importantly a voracious reader. In between shots, she always kept reading books. In his younger days, my father was the biggest fan of her mother Tanuja, and he says he told Kajol the same. In Marathi, she said *Mag tumhala bhetwayla pahije majhya aaila* which means I should get you to meet my mother in that case.

My father recalls an incident from the movie *Raakh,* directed by Basu Bhattacharya's son. He played Aamir Khan's father in this film and in one scene he had to slap his son. Now in movies, the slaps are only in the air. But Aamir Khan who is a dedicated actor who is immersed in his roles suggested to my Dad to give him a real tight slap which would bring out the right emotions in both of them. My father says this was not easy for sure.

Narsimha was a movie with Dimple Kapadia as the main lead. In one of the scenes that my father shot with her where he is giving her some advice, he managed to give a great shot in just one take. Dimple was so impressed with the shot that she just hugged him and said how brilliant was that. The funny part is that all junior artists and other members of the production crew thought that the hug was a part of the shot advised by the Director. Dimple naturally developed a respect for my father during the course of the shoot. That day after the scene was shot, she overheard my father telling Director N Chandra, that he had to rush to Shivaji Mandir Auditorium at Dadar for his play *Wada*

Narsimha

Chirebandi which was at 4 pm. It was already 3 pm by then. Dimple simply instructed her driver to drop him there. Such was the impact he had created in that one scene he had shot with her that day.

"Angaar" marked another milestone in his career, recommended by both Om Puri and Nana Patekar to director Shashilal Nair. This turned out to be one of the most interesting characters my father has ever played in any film. He met Director Shashilal Nair, who liked him immediately and cast him as Jackie Shroff's father. Surprisingly, the scriptwriter hadn't written any lines for his character. Mr. Nair told my father to create his own dialogues, which he did. All the dialogues he speaks in the film are his own creations. In the movie, he often calls out to his son Jackie as "Ey Jaggu Jaggu" in his unique style, which became hugely popular. People started recognizing him by this nickname wherever he went - airports, railway stations, and markets. Even Jackie Shroff began calling him "Baba" during the film shoot and continued to do so, showing respect even at my parents' 50th wedding anniversary party in 2012.

Angaar

With directors Shashilal Nair and Govind Nihalani

Guests loved seeing their playful interactions. After the film's success, Shashilal Nair complimented my father and said that probably his role was the best-played role in the film.

After *Angaar's* whopping success at the box office, my father got a call from RK Films requesting him to meet Rishi Kapoor at his residence. He met Mr. Kapoor and instantly bagged a role in the film *Aa Ab Laut Chale.* The role required him to travel to the USA. Visas etc. were organized by the unit and my father left for his first-ever trip to America. He remembers the Kapoor hospitality right from the airport till his return. Food and liquor always flowed at the hotels where the crew stayed after the day's shoot was over. Ranbir Kapoor was very young then and my father remembers how he assisted him on the smallest of matters, without any attitude. He was just like any other assistant and with no aura or attitude of being the Director's son on the sets. One day they were shooting along the streets of New Jersey.

My father's scene was with Paresh Rawal and there were the locals on the streets watching the shoot. They called out *Ey Jaggu Jaggu* on seeing him. It was an awesome feeling for my father to be so well recognized and appreciated even in the USA for his role in Angaar. Paresh Rawal said to him "*Arey bhai wah, aapko tow sab jaanteyhai yaha*"(everyone seems to know you here). A similar incident occurred when Sanjay Dutt was jailed, and a lot of popular actors joined in support of him in a procession in Bandra. There were *Jaggu Jaggu* shouts then too by the watchers. Johnny Lever the comedian said to my Father "*Wow I have never received such a response anywhere*".

A Director from the South, Late T. S. Ranga saw some of these films and approached my father for a role in his upcoming Hindi film *Giddh.* This was in 1984. The film had Smita Patil and Om Puri in the main roles and was based on the Devadasi system prevalent in Karnataka. The shooting happened in Hubli and on a set made on the outskirts of Bangalore. My father played a major negative role in this film, of the Zamindar who exploits young girls who are Devadasis. The impact of his negative role was such that one of the articles in the media commended his acting and said that no young girl would want to come anywhere near him after seeing this film. In film shoots, it's common for actors not to be present together during scenes. Directors often film one actor's part first and then the other's, combining them in editing. However, in a particularly intense and lengthy scene where my father had to confront Smita Patil, he asked her to be there during his part. As a theatre actor,

Giddh

this made him more comfortable, and she kindly agreed. The scene turned out well with both actors performing together.

During the shooting of "Giddh," the cast stayed at the residence of the Industries Minister of Karnataka, a friend of the director. Meals were usually South Indian vegetarian, which my father and Nana Patekar sometimes missed. After shoots, they would buy chicken and eggs, and Nana would cook them in the house.My father's Boss Late Deep Bhojwani organized a special show for the then Director(Marketing) of Indianoil, Late BK Bakshi at a theatre in Dadar, Mumbai. Smita Patil herself attended this show at my father's request. The film had requested a tax exemption certificate being a public service theme of creating awareness about malpractices, but sadly did not get it. Several screenings were done on television at later dates and the film is now available for viewing on Amazon Prime and Zee. Had it been a success at the box office, my father would have been at some other level perhaps

Rihaai was another interesting film that my father acted in. It had Vinod Khanna, and Hema Malini in the lead. It was a film based on the lives of carpenters from central India who left their homes to reside in metros. The film was directed by Aruna Desai and was shot on the outskirts of Bhuj in Gujarat. The cast lived in different small houses taken on rent and my father shared a house with actor Harish Patel. An interesting incident from this film was when my father was expected to take part in a dance sequence in this film. He was super nervous about dancing as that was not something that came easily to him. When the shoot of this dance sequence was happening in Mumbai, my father was busy shooting for Shyam Benegal's TV serial *Bharat ek Khoj* and hence could not attend it. Arunaji later called him to Famous Studio and got him to dance individually and later patched that shot with the main dance at the editing table. In the film, one does see him dancing in that song alongside the main lead Hema Malini.

Parineeta was the next big film where he played a major role as Vidya Balan's uncle whose house is mortgaged in the film. It was an important character in the storyline. This film was directed by the late Pradip Sarkar and the shoot was done in Kolkata. I remember my mother had for the first time accompanied my father on any shoot. Both were away for a month. My mother was a teacher at Bai Avabai Framji Petit Girls High School at Pali Hill Bandra in Mumbai and her summer vacations were on at that time. Vidya Balan's mother had accompanied her on this shoot and over the month-long period, my mother and she became good friends. Later when I met Vidya when she was the Chief guest at my Lavasa Women's Drive award function in March

Parineeta

2013, she had fond memories of those Kolkata days with my parents. My father says Vidya's makeup man was called Vidyadhar so he would call his own makeup man Achyutdhar. That had become a popular joke on the sets then.

Many films and several cameo roles in big movies kept coming one after another. My father had the privilege of working with two of his all-time favorite greats, Dilip Kumar and Amitabh Bachchan, in "Quila" and "Bhootnath."

One of the most memorable roles that my father

Bhoothnath

played was that of a professor in *3 Idiots*. It was only one major scene in the film but perhaps the most iconic. A film by Raju Hirani, it has become one of the classic and timeless movies in public memory. My father's scene was shot at the IIT campus in Mumbai. His dialogue *Kehna kya chahte ho* in the scene where he asks Aamir Khan for the definition of a machine has become an ever-popular line. Several years after the film's release in December 2009. It remains in public memory. To date, memes, gifs, and other creative formats of this scene with my father saying *Kehna kya chahte ho* are used by people and used in comical contexts all over digital media. It has truly become a timeless asset belonging to my father for times to come. It will etch him in the sands of time by remaining on the internet and in people's minds.

3 idiots

In 2016, my father acted in a Marathi film for the first time in a significant role. The film was titled *Ventilator.* Although a Maharashtrian, for some reason, my father was always invited by Hindi filmmakers more than Marathi. This film was a delight for him as he simply loved working with the young Director Rajesh Mhapuskar, who also shared similar love and respect for him.

In 2017, my father got a call from Sanjay Leela Bhansali's office requesting him to meet the Director at his residence. He met him and was immediately signed up for his next film which required him to shoot abroad. It was the highest fee he would get for any role. However, the film was deferred and later shelved when the director had a major difference of opinion with the hero of the film. Maybe there were more reasons for the film to not go on the floors, but my father certainly lost out on a good opportunity with a great director.

In summary, his Bollywood journey spanned four decades. His career came to a close in 2022 at the age of eighty-eight due to age and health reasons. He is satisfied

Vijeta

Tezaab

Suraksha

Lage raho Munnabhai

Dilwale

with his accomplishments, having earned everything on his merit, without seeking favors for roles. He truly experiences *samadhaan* with all the love and respect that the public has given him from time to time. Today, I feel proud when I hear anyone and everyone who sees his photo making this consistent remark: "*Wow what a fine actor. He is so simple and natural*"

My father has acted in over 125 films.The list of films is appended at the end of this book

■ ■ ■

17

A familiar face on television: Lifetime Achievement Award from Zee TV

Thanks to Sulabha Deshpande's recommendation, Director Satish Alekar contacted my father for his first role in television serials in 1985. The serial was *Dekho Magar Pyaar Se.* Thus began a successful journey in the world of television with several serials one after the other. He has been a familiar face on television for over 3 decades. *Wagle ki Duniya, Mahanagar, Bharat Ek Khoj, Nukkad, Mriganayni, Parampara, Agle Janam mohe bitiyahi kijo, Thodisi Zameen Thhodasa Aasmaan* and several more. Most of them became extremely

successful. Several of these serials were directed by eminent people like Shyam Benegal, Vijaya Mehta, Amol Palekar, Basu Chatterjee, etc. He also appeared

in notable roles in shows produced by Doordarshan. Some of these included "Gajra," "Daakghar," "Birbal," "Pratibha ani Pratima," and "Raktabeej."

His last stint with television was in 2022 with the Marathi serial "Maza Hoshil Na" on Zee Marathi, where his role as the jovial yet forgetful patriarch, Appa, resonated deeply with Marathi audiences. Much of the series was filmed at a bungalow in Yeoor Hills, Thane. Since 2017, my father has been living with me following my mother's illness. And the set of this serial was hardly 2 km from my home in Thane. The three young producers of this serial Omkar Kate, Sujay Hande, and Subodh Khanolkar gave my father love and respect of a very high order. Sending him a vehicle with an escort for pick up and drop to the set, celebrating his birthdays on sets or at my home, shooting his scenes at home, and then patching it up in the serial to avoid his travel during Covid and several such respectful gestures got my father very attached to all folks of this unit. On his eighty-ninth birthday, the crew and cast of this serial did an online video call to wish him. Some members came home with a customized Old Monk bottle and a cake. This was the most pleasant surprise of his life. The production team of this serial, Ocean Films, have got so fond of him and his happy self, that to date they come over to our house and shoot short reels with him. A short series on Instagram was made in February 2024, titled *Old Monk Says*. It is a funny satirical dig at the attitudes of the youth of today.

The role of Appa in "Maza Hoshil Na" was my father's final major acting role because, by 2022, his legs and knees had weakened considerably, making shooting on sets increasingly challenging. The COVID-19 pandemic exacerbated concerns, especially after senior actors like Ashalata Wabgaonkar passed away due to the virus. Globally, there was a reluctance among producers and directors to cast actors over seventy, and at eighty-eight, my father faced a complete halt in role offers post-COVID. Despite ongoing audition requests, once his age was known, producers hesitated to take the risk. But the grand finale was truly fulfilling when he got the **Lifetime Achievement Award** from Zee Marathi in 2021. We decided to give him a surprise. The Ocean Films team had informed me that my father was chosen for the Award. My father never attended any functions usually. I somehow managed to coax him into coming with me for the same. It was a touching moment for

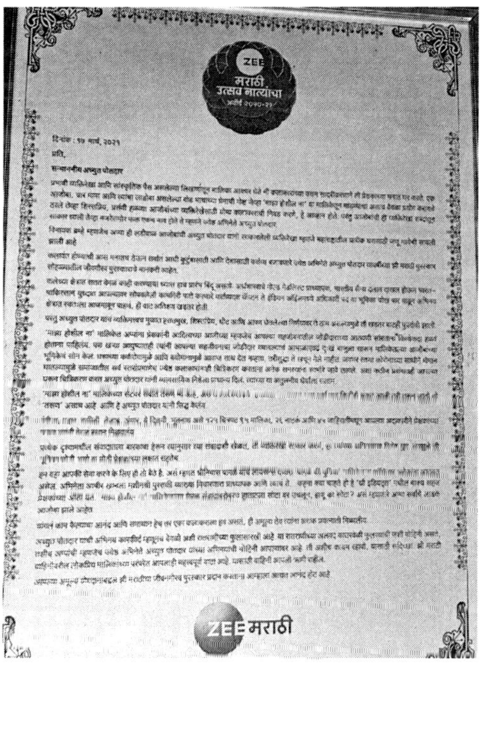

all of us when his name was announced and he went up on stage to receive his award. He needed a little help to go up and also a chair to sit and speak as he could not stand for too long. For the first time, a man who would host programs all his life was speechless with the contentment he experienced from this recognition. We had mixed emotions. There were tears of joy in our eyes as we stood up along with all the attendees to give him respectful applause and also a silent sadness to see our father not so agile anymore.

Throughout his career, my father also appeared in advertisements for numerous prominent brands such as McDonald's, LIC, Fevicol, Maggi, Bajaj, Parachute oil, Fair and Lovely, Safola oil, IPL Jio, Paytm, and HDFC amongst many more. Director Pradeep Sorcar, in particular, held him in high regard, and my father worked on nearly ten ads with him.

Apart from acting, he gained popularity for his hosting skills too. He was popularly invited to host various

Indian Oil programs, especially music shows. Even after retiring from the Company in 1992, he continued to host music shows at the Indian Oil premises in Bandra East, Mumbai for several years. I have fond memories of attending three such shows featuring Pandit Bhimsen Joshi, Pandit Hariprasad

A familiar face on television: Lifetime Achievement Award from Zee TV

Chaurasia, and Smt. Kishori Amonkar. His quick wit, eloquence, and ability to engage with the audience made him a sought-after host, and he was loved for his witty remarks and spontaneous banter.

My father has acted in over 95 Hindi television serials, 25 Marathi serials, and 20 Doordarshan programs. He has appeared in over 45 ads of leading brands and has done another twenty ads with just his voiceover. The list is appended at the end of this book.

■ ■ ■

18

The joy of giving: Social contributions

My father dislikes the terms "charity" or "donations," feeling they may diminish the dignity of the recipient. He therefore uses the word contribution. He says that is because it is aimed at helping the receiver move ahead in his endeavor. This belief stems from his childhood when his mother had taught him that sixteen percent of one's income should be dedicated to social welfare, a principle he held onto throughout his life.

The Indian Oil income was just sufficient to take care of family welfare. Therefore, when he started getting some additional income from his acting endeavors, he decided to give away not just sixteen percent, but ALL the income generated from his acting pursuits for a social cause. Being a Maharashtrian, he had often observed, that the Maharashtra Mandals across the country were not as well funded as those of some other communities. For some reason, the Marathi man has always been low on the contribution aspect. Probably because most Maharashtrians were usually salaried and without deep pockets. Or maybe it was just a cultural thing too. I don't know. The Indore Marathi Samaj was founded in 1989 and his friend Mr. Rahtekar had once called him to invite some contribution. My father instantly contributed Rs 25,000 in the name of his deceased parents, whose names are now honored in the main hall of the Samaj premises.

He never looked back after this first contribution. He decided to contribute all his acting-generated income to Maharashtra Mandals across India to encourage and strengthen them. He started with his hometown Indore. It became a passionate personal project for him thereafter to give large contributions to over 70 Marathi Mandals across India based in 52 cities. Contributions were made to promote youngsters in the fields of art and culture, especially theatre. He made a list of all his near and dear ones who had departed. This included his family members, friends, and also actors and directors that he revered. He then called up several Maharashtra Mandals across India and started sending them contributions proactively in the names of the deceased. To date, all the Mandals are running these contributions actively. In some places it is being given away as annual

नईदुनिया
सिटीलाइव
'इसलिए कमा रहा हूं ताकि युवाओं को प्रमोट कर सकूं'
शहर आए फिल्म, सीरियल और रंगमंच के वरिष्ठ कलाकार अच्युत पोतदार से खास गुफ्तगू

awards and in others it is scholarships. Each award and scholarship is named after one of the persons suggested by my father. He has given lump sums to every Mandal and the interest from those fixed deposits is what the Mandals use annually for awards and scholarships.

Pandit Satydev Dubey, Shri PL Deshpande, Dr Shriram Lagu, Sulbha Deshpande, and every single departed family member are some of the names for the awards and scholarships across the country. There came a time when the number of contributions started exceeding the number of deceased friends and family members. So, he started contributing in the names of the living family members and friends too. Large contributions were also made to Shri Baba Amte's Anandvan and some other NGOs in the country

My father is a low-key, humble, and simple person who quietly went about his charitable work without seeking recognition. So much so, that he did not share details even with us, his family. One day, around ten years back, we saw a very neatly done-up file called Samadhaan: The Joy of Giving. When we went through it, we realized how large-hearted he is to give away all that he earned from acting. We realized that it was almost all of his earnings through acting over four decades that he had happily given away. This was indeed a remarkable and selfless act of dedicating his earnings to benefit others.

A simple man with a large heart, he says that after everything that he did or achieved in life, this joy of giving gave him his ultimate true *Samadhaan.*

■ ■ ■

19

Health: A story of resilience and boundless courage

I shall not use the words health setbacks because health problems never set him back.

He remembers his earliest health issue was when he was a child. He would get a very high fever every year, which would come every alternate day and last a fortnight. This pattern lasted a few years till he became a teenager. One Dr. R. W. Apte in Martand Chowk Indore would treat him. The fever was called Ekantara. The next issue arose when he appeared in 1953 for the Air Force fighter pilot exam. They found traces of albumin in his blood, and he was rejected as a result. His health was very good till 1976 when one day he had severe pain in his stomach at Nagpur. The pain was severe and lasted several days. One Dr. Kolwadkar detected it as peptic ulcers and treated him. This was followed by the development of piles in 1987. It was at some wedding in Indore, that he realized he had developed bleeding piles. An officer who worked with him in Indian Oil, Mr. Mukherjee suggested that instead of going to any Doctor, if he sincerely ate radish twice a day with his meals and reduced spices, his piles would vanish. A sincere disciplined man that my father is, he did this religiously for a few years and the piles indeed disappeared without leaving a trace. He had taken no medicine.

In 2001, my parents had gone visiting my mother's maternal home in Jhansi. My father had returned to Mumbai earlier and my mother had stayed back for a few days for some reason. On 2nd March, 2001, my father experienced a heart attack while no one was home. Despite the intense pain and profuse sweating, he managed to descend four flights of stairs from our fourth-floor apartment in Bandra Reclamation, Mumbai, where there was no elevator. With Lilavati Hospital just a few buildings away, he tried to hail a rickshaw on the street, but none would take him such a short distance. He then sought help from our ground-floor neighbor, whose son promptly drove him to the hospital. There, he underwent his first angioplasty. Exactly a year later, on March 2, 2002, he suffered a second heart attack and underwent a subsequent angioplasty at Lilavati Hospital, performed by Dr. Nitin Gokhale and Dr. Vijan.

In 2005, he developed a slipped disc and received aggressive physiotherapy at Lilavati Hospital, which initially helped him recover. However, the problem recurred in 2007, necessitating surgery. Although three operations were initially recommended, he responded well to the first surgery and did not require further procedures.

In 2009, my father experienced a mild stroke while visiting Indore, causing weakness and numbness on one side of his body. Recognizing the symptoms, we rushed him back to Mumbai where he received treatment at Lilavati Hospital under Dr. Nitin Gokhale, his cardiologist. Through physiotherapy and his determination, he recovered well from both, the stroke and the previous slipped disc issues, which could have both been debilitating. It was his strong willpower and of course, the grace of God that helped him heal fully.

Then in 2012, during a routine health checkup, doctors discovered that his pulse rate was alarmingly high at 177 beats per minute. The cardiologist at Lilavati Hospital recommended shock treatment to stabilize his heart rhythm and he was admitted to Asian Heart Hospital. However, our family friend and cardiologist, Dr. Rane intervened just as my father was about to undergo the procedure. He felt it unnecessary and potentially risky. Despite the medical advice, my father showed his fearless attitude, questioning us why the procedure wasn't being performed as planned. My father was feeling more irritation than relief at the unexpected change of plans. It was so funny.

In 2015, a significant challenge arose when my father began experiencing hoarseness in his voice, his most valued asset. After consulting Dr. Pusalkar at Lilavati Hospital, a biopsy was done which revealed localized cancer in his larynx, termed cancer in-situ. Due to the tumor's inaccessible location in his throat, surgical removal was deemed impractical. I used to work at Piramal Enterprises in those days and Anand Piramal suggested we meet Dr. Sultan Pradhan, the renowned head and neck onco-surgeon. Dr. Pradhan examined him and said he would try operating. However, on the day of the operation, he came out of the operation theatre saying the tumor was inaccessible and accessing it could damage the surroundings. We were then advised to give him radiation therapy to regress the growth. I moved my parents to my home in Thane in August 2015 as Jupiter Hospital was next door. Dr. R. Bhalawat was a renowned onco-radiologist there. The treatment was started. My father endured 3 months of suffering with the skin of his throat burnt nearly black with radiation. Eating and drinking had become a problem and a rice tube had to be inserted through the nose to feed him a liquid diet. However, his positive attitude and willpower healed him, and he became cancer-free very soon. The fearless man then showed his true colors of courage to the oncologist. Just for perspective, my father had started chewing tobacco at age sixteen and drinking around age twenty. Daily drinking Rum had started at age thirty. After three months of radiation, when he went for his follow-up, he told the Doctor that he wanted to restart his tobacco and his daily drink. My mother and all of us were angry that even after fighting throat cancer, he still wanted to consume what was forbidden. But finally, on his insistence, the oncologist and all of us decided to let him live the rest of his life on his terms and not put any restrictions. Fortunately, he has always been a controlled drinker and he also brought down his tobacco consumption to twice a day ever since.

By 2020, my father's heart began experiencing bouts of tachycardia, indicating an irregular heart rhythm. Dr. Nabar in Thane recommended a pacemaker, but at 86 years old, my father decided against any further invasive procedures. He chose instead to manage his heart condition with medications and his indomitable willpower. Despite a brief encounter with COVID-19 in 2021, he recovered swiftly. In December 2022, when I was away in the United States with my daughter and sister's family, he developed acute acidity, vomited blood, and passed blood in his stools. It was worrisome. His cardiologist assured us on the phone that we need not rush back and that he would manage him. The phoenix arose again with God's grace. After that episode, he collapsed thrice with hypoxia, which means low oxygen, and was hospitalized. In December 2023, he told us that he would never wish to get hospitalized again.

Throughout his life, my father has demonstrated fearlessness and courage, placing immense trust in his doctors, which has consistently aided his rapid recovery from various health challenges.

■ ■ ■

20

My mother Asha: The wind beneath his wings

My mother Asha Potdar was a simple and sweet person. She married my father on 6th May 1962, when she was just about to turn 21. She was born and brought up in Jhansi and was the second child of Dr Vishnu Damodar Dhulekar and his wife Indirabai

Wife Asha

Dhulekar. It was a joint family, and my mother grew up in a very comfortable and loving atmosphere where everyone was soft-spoken and kind. Her father was a practicing Ayurvedic doctor and so were her two brothers, uncles, and cousins. Her granduncle Raghunathrao Dhulekar, a freedom fighter and a member of Parliament in the first assembly after independence, had founded the Bundelkhand Ayurvedic College in Jhansi and her father was the principal of this college. The Dhulekar family was an influential, well-respected family in Jhansi. My mother married into the Potdar family, which was radically different from the Dhulekars. The Potdars were mostly teachers by profession and much louder and dominating in disposition. My father had already advised my mother before marriage that his mother and his sister would have to be respected as they came first in his life and were both single women now. My mother diligently followed all my father's instructions. Not once in her married life of 57 years, did she raise her voice or say a word against her in-laws. She maintained harmony and good relations with one and all.

My mother was a mature, calm,and kind woman. She was not materialistic at all. Simple sarees and little to no jewelry except her mangalsutra were her typical person. I do not remember her ever making any demands on my father. She looked elegant and striking, with a dusky complexion and sharp features. In her younger days, because of her hairline and sharp nose, a lot of people found some resemblance with actress Waheeda Rehman. Popularly their friends called my parents Guru Dutt and Waheeda Rehman. Mother had a lovely voice and she had learned some music in her childhood at Jhansi. She would sing Madan Mohan songs at the insistence of my father's colleagues at Army parties. She knew knitting and would make lovely sweaters in those days. At my father's suggestion, she went ahead and did higher education, and got her B. Ed. degree in 1973 from Jhansi, when her three children were just five, three, and one year old.

She was also very courageous. She lived alone in blackouts at Pathankot when my father was away during the Indo-Pak war. She had a few miscarriages but never lost hope or complained. She stayed with her mother-in-law and sister-in-law when my father was away and was the ideal daughter-in-law. She supported my father in all his endeavors, starting from his decision to join the Indian Army right after they got married. She continued to support every decision he made. My father was always the decision-maker in the family. My mother was a dedicated wife who willingly took a supportive role in maintaining peace and harmony in our home.

In 1985, she began teaching at Bai Avabai Framji Petit Girls High School in Bandra, Mumbai, where she worked until her retirement in 2002.She was loved by all her students. Most of the students in this school were children of film stars, given that it was a Pali Hill neighborhood. To supplement our household income, my mother contributed all her earnings, both from her salary and tuition to my father, who managed their finances.

She was fond of gardening, and she kept the home meticulously neat and clean. A great cook, she always kept her husband, children, and her five grandchildren delightfully happy with her awesome preparations. Her *daal* and her *rice kheer* were the family favorites. She was also an artist and had made several beautiful paintings in oil and watercolors on canvas as well as on glass.

She raised us with love and never once raised her voice or hand to us. Our father was strict and disciplined, and she respected his authority by not spoiling us when he was upset. Nevertheless, we always felt her comforting presence and love whenever we needed it. She was a respectful and non-intrusive person, allowing everyone their own space. Unlike the typical mother who might excessively dote on her children or husband, she became our closest friend as we grew up and started families of our own. Over the years, all three of us naturally gravitated more towards her. She never interfered in our new families after our marriages and was always silently and gracefully there for us if and when we needed it.

My mother was a healthy woman all along. I do not remember her taking ill during my growing up years. She was diagnosed with Diabetes and High blood pressure in 1997. This was detected when she came back from Jhansi after her mother passed away. In 2002, she had a near death experience when her gall bladder had to be removed and there were some post-operative complications. This was followed by knee replacement surgery in 2010.

I could sense a sea change in her disposition after 2010. She had started feeling low, largely because of her health issues. Maybe the cancer had started taking root by then? It was detected only in 2017. It was a day of gloom for all of us when that news was broken to us. It was November 2017, and my sister had come down from London to celebrate Diwali with us at my place in Thane. We all had a wonderful reunion and later drove with my late husband Shirish to our farmhouse in Talegao. That day, my mother was especially happy. The day after returning from Talegao, my sister suggested my mother visit a local doctor in Kandivali for a general health check-up, including checking her blood pressure. There was no particular reason, perhaps just intuition. During the check-up, my mother's blood pressure reading was alarmingly high at 230/120. The doctor, surprised by the reading, checked it multiple times and advised immediate hospitalization. We rushed my mother to Lilavati Hospital, where she was admitted to the ICU. During a chest X-ray prompted by unusual sounds the doctor heard with a stethoscope, they discovered a large tumor in her lungs. A biopsy confirmed our worst fears: she had stage 3B Adenocarcinoma of the lungs. Despite feeling tired for a few months, she had shown no symptoms of lung cancer. Her fatigue had been attributed to her diabetes and long-standing anemia.

Our hearts shattered. It felt like the world was collapsing around us. We cried until there were no tears left, praying desperately for a miracle. We found a glimmer of hope when oncologist Dr. Ramakant Deshpande recommended a gene mutation test on the tumor sample, which turned out positive. Certain genes had indeed mutated, leading to the development of cancer in an otherwise benign woman. She received medications that were effective globally for cancers based on gene mutations. However, her delicate body couldn't tolerate these strong medicines, causing severe diarrhea that persisted despite efforts to manage it. Eventually, we had to discontinue the medications, and she began losing weight rapidly. We tried Tibetan medicines from Dharmasala, but unfortunately, they didn't provide relief. Her condition continued to decline.

What was remarkable about her was her unwavering strength and positivity throughout this ordeal. She never once broke down or spoke negatively. Innocently, she would ask if the tumor could be surgically removed, and upon hearing it wasn't accessible, she would simply smile and accept her fate gracefully. She had already come to terms with death in her mind, never shedding a tear or expressing anxiety, so as not to burden her worried family.

On 7th May 2019, at the age of seventy-seven, she passed away from cancer. It happened to be her 57th wedding anniversary according to the Hindu calendar and the auspicious day of Akshaye Tritiya. On that day, a pure and gentle soul ascended to heaven. My father was with me when my mother took her last breath. I was holding one hand and he was holding the other, when her breath finally said goodbye to her body. My father could not bear the loss of his "One woman" who had stood by him like a rock of Gibraltar for all 57 years of their married life. Every night for nearly four years after her death, he would cry and feel overwhelmed with sadness. He keeps her photo by his bed and believes she is always with him. He hopes to take his last breath in the same bed in my home where she took hers.

I consider myself a truly blessed daughter as my mother passed away resting her head on my hand. Her positive spirit remains in my home always, to guide and protect me. This feeling of her constant presence gives me immense joy and confidence.

Since the time my mother was diagnosed with cancer in November 2017, both my parents had been living with me. Just as we were preparing for my mother's passing, another tragedy struck. My husband, Shirish, suddenly passed away from severe dengue fever on November 29, 2018. He was only fifty-five years old. It was a major setback for us and came unexpectedly. My children and I were in a state of shock at his sudden demise but I had to get stronger. I still had my mother to look after, and my children to look after, and also complete a lot of unfinished tasks for Shirish.

My ninety-year-old aunt Akka, my father's sister, hadalso passed away a few days before Shirish, in the same month. Akka had been a guardian to both my children in their childhood and I had become her guardian in her old age. My mother's health was declining rapidly by this time. So, it was a very difficult time for our family as we faced three deaths back to back in six months.

After my mother passed away on May 7, 2019, my father was all set to go back to his home in Kandivali. But I couldn't bear to let my father stay alone in Kandivali so urged him to stay with me. I had lost my husband at the same time and needed his moral support as much as he needed mine. He agreed and has been living with me ever since. Around the same time, my brother Amrish was also going through a divorce so he moved in with us too. I feel truly blessed to have had both my father and brother with me during such a challenging period, after losing both my mother and my husband.

■ ■ ■

21

Strong values, simple living

My father and mother both lived a very simple life. I have never seen my father own more than 4 shirts and 2 trousers at any given point in time. Simple nutritious food, simple clothes, occasional outings and holidays, and a focus on education were the sum and substance of our life with our parents before marriage. And these values have continued with us to date. There was never any aspiration that I ever saw in my father for bigger houses, better cars, or exotic experiences. This was despite exposure to the glamourous film and television industry and after living in the fancy

neighborhood of Pali Hill. As we grew up and entered the corporate world, we sometimes found our father's approach to simple living amusing. He would carry sofas, Godrej cupboards, bedsheets, trunks, and other items from one house to the next instead of buying new ones. He believed strongly in spending money wisely and avoiding unnecessary expenses. All his savings went into fixed deposits in one bank, and he avoided investing in stocks. His real estate investments were basic and planned for a simple retirement lifestyle.

My father lived all through his work life in the official accommodation. He bought his own house after retirement in Bandra Reclamation in 1993 from where he moved to Kandivali East in 2004. Both the homes were compact and in modest societies. His simplicity and minimalistic frugal living were exemplified when he took all the things he had been carrying with him for decades and used them again in the final abode that he had chosen for himself and his wife. Needless to say, the maintenance and cleanliness quotients of my parents were so high that everything still looked fresh and good. Their curtains were so well maintained that they lasted long. There were limited new investments they made in the new house.

Despite his frugal habits, my father was never stingy. He was known for his kindness and generosity, making voluntary contributions whenever possible. His life philosophy was to live minimally, which he embodied in his thoughts, words, and actions.

I remember that his day would start with a cup of tea with very little sugar. He never had breakfast. He always liked simple home-cooked food made by my mother. He hated adding sugar or jaggery to food, which was a custom in typical Marathi Brahmin households. He loved reading and made sure we read newspapers daily. He bought Maharashtra Times and Indian Express. He sent us to Convent schools to learn good English, which he believed was crucial in a competitive world. He also wanted us to speak pure Marathi, our mother tongue, which is why he bought the Marathi paper. He admired Arun Shourie's writing style and viewpoints, so he regularly bought Indian Express, where Shourie was the editor. After retiring, he had more time to read and would visit Ideal Book Depot in Dadar, Mumbai, and would buy around fifty Marathi books at a time, often autobiographies or biographies. About ten years ago, when he finished reading them all and his small home in Kandivali was filling up, he generously gifted them to people who wanted them.

He has always been fastidious about cleanliness and order. Wearing chappals 24 hours at home, not keeping wet towels on the bed, keeping things correctly in each section of the refrigerator as per the logic he had explained, immaculate cupboard stacking with no creases, neatly laid out footwear, no creases on bedsheets or sofas were amongst the hundreds of teachings he gave us. How to take messages on the phone, make lists of things to do, neat handwriting and filing, write down expenses, and give back people's utensils immediately were some more things he taught us, and which remain with all three of us to date. My father always emphasized doing everything perfectly. His motto for us was "Kaam perfect." This perfectionist attitude in all three of us likely came from his strict values and disciplined upbringing. He believed in keeping files up-to-date and organized so that they could be easily found even during a power outage.

He had a routine for paying maids and service providers like the milkman and car cleaner on the last day of the month instead of the first day of the next month. I remember their salaries were prepared neatly with a small note clipped to each bundle stating the name, amount, and date. These were placed on the dining table the day before payday, ensuring timely payments. In our home, a Kalnirnay calendar in the lobby detailed laundry schedules and important dates marked with notes. There was also a notebook with neatly written phone numbers from the days of landlines. He insisted on everything having its designated place, becoming upset if something was misplaced.

Since his youth, my father has maintained a daily personal diary, a habit he continues to this day. Recently, when we cleared out his house in Kandivali to rent it out, we found over 50 of his diaries. I asked if we could keep a few and discard the rest, which he reluctantly agreed to after initially refusing. I later felt sad and guilty for suggesting it. Those diaries held his memories and experiences so carefully preserved, and I had treated them so thoughtlessly.

My father was always strict with us but at the same time, he was also very liberal and progressive. This was a very unique facet of his person. He allowed all three of us to choose our careers and our life partners, which was quite unconventional for a strict parent who might usually have micromanaged these decisions. I remember my father would spank my brother when he failed in Mathematics at school. But when my brother excelled (after getting tutoring from Pol Master)my proud father celebrated by distributing sweets to the entire building. He repeated this joyous gesture when my brother achieved a first-class result in standard 12. Similarly, when my sister faced a divorce in 1999 at a very young age, he supported her decision, assuring her that he would always be there for her.

Another very unique facet of my father and even my mother is that whilst both of them were raised in strict Brahmin households, they have been so modern and progressive that when each one of us chose our partners, he did not ask their castes. Till today he does not know which caste all our spouses belong to. How rare are they! I remember two of my friends who were boys, but not my boyfriends, had written me a few letters from their hostels. In those days, there were no phones so as good friends they had shared anecdotes from newfound hostel life through a few letters. My father opened one or two and realized from the tone that there was nothing he needed to worry about. After that, he would give the letters unopened. His faith and trust has made us children always walk on the right paths in life.

My father did not believe in jewelry or investing in gold for his daughters' marriages which is a norm usually. He firmly believed that his daughters were jewels and would be assets to any family they married into. He had raised them well with strong values and ensured that they were financially independent. I remember him telling us often that the true ornament is in our brains and is not the one worn on the body. My mother was simple too, so she never challenged any of his thought processes or actions, including this one. As a result, we never bought gold, even at the festival of Dhanteras. My mother never wore gold beyond the mangalsutra and a simple bangle and earrings that she had made at Jhansi all through her life. The first piece of jewelry ever bought in our house was at the time of my wedding and that too because my mother said it wouldn't look nice if their girl had no jewelry at all. Hence in one go, in early 1992, I remember all of us going to a jeweler in Bandra and my father purchased 3 sets each for my mother and his two daughters. Each set contained one necklace, one set of earrings, one ring, and one bangle.

When my sister Aparna told my father that Vicky (my brother-in-law) who was in London then, had proposed to her a couple of years after her divorce, my father gave her the go-ahead and simply said 'If it goes wrong this time,you should just come home.' Since he did not believe in rituals, we all had court marriages. But when Vicky's mother expressed the desire to have an Arya Samaj marriage for her only son after the court marriage, my father obliged as for him, this was a mother's wish, and he equates 'mother to God'. He immediately agreed to have the marriage with rituals.

All three of us chose our partners and succeeded in our careers, with our father giving us unwavering support and having pride in our independence. He is delighted to see us thriving on our own. With his five grandchildren, he's remarkably liberal, never meddling in their lives. While he's not the traditional doting grandfather who spoils them, he is always encouraging and open with the younger generation.

Recently whilst writing this book, when I asked him what his unmet dreams were, he said there were none. But when I nudged him, he said that he certainly had the potential to become an Executive Director at Indianoil, a Brigadier in the Indian Army, or a much bigger actor in the film industry. He says luck did not favor him and he created enemies because of his acumen as well as his integrity. He was simple and candid and did not feel the need to flatter anyone. He did not market himself in the film industry nor did he become part of any coterie. All this prevented his growth in every profession that he undertook. Nevertheless, he has no regrets in his life.

My father's value systems have always been very strong. Integrity, Honesty, Discipline, Perfection, Simplicity, Fearlessness, Contentment, and Positive thinking have been the driving factors of his life to date. He sums up his life with the word *Samadhaan.*

■ ■ ■

22

Family, friends, and associates

My father was the 10th among 11 siblings born to my grandparents. Today, none of his brothers or sisters are alive. He greatly admired his elder brother, Madhavji Potdar, who was his earliest role model and source of guidance in life. His brother-in-law, Prabhakarrao Kibe, fondly known as Kibesaheb, played a significant role in sparking my father's interest in acting. He was a musician and a talented mimic.

Best friend Narayan

Narayan Joshi was my father's best friend. He was nearest and dearest to him. Their friendship dates back to 1942 when both of them moved into Martand Chowk. Whilst our house was numbered 22, Narayan Joshi's house was numbered 9. It was a beautiful house with a large terrace and warm vibes. He was the only child of his parents. Narayan's father had once invited most local neighborhood boys of his age for a *Shravani* ceremony. In this ceremony, all the boys whose *Munja* had been done would undergo a thread-changing ritual. That's where my father met him for the first time. They became best friends ever since. Narayan taught my father to cycle and then to ride a scooter and then a car. Both started learning violin together but whilst my father gave up after three years, Narayan went ahead and became a very good player of the violin. He would often play on the radio.

We fondly called him Baba and his wife whose name is Malti Joshi was named Mamuni by me when I was a toddler stammering for words. They became like second parents to us due to the deep bond they shared with my parents. Baba and Mamuni visited us often. Baba was the calmest, most gentle, and peace-loving person I have ever known. Always smiling and appreciative, he would often compliment others with a heartfelt "Wah." He had a strong affinity for technology and was our go-to person for gadget repairs, and was greatly admired by my father for his skills in this area. He worked in Iran for a few years, but most of his career was spent at a company called Hico in India. Fortunately, the company's head office was very close to our house in Mahim, so we would often see Baba during those days.

My father and Baba did several trips together with their wives. One of their fondest memories was their trip to Kashmir in 1966, which my father describes as a true

*With Narayan &
Malti Joshi*

honeymoon for both couples. Sadly, Baba passed away peacefully on August 19, 2022, after a short illness. My father was devastated; losing his closest friend and confidante so soon after losing his beloved wife in 2019 changed him profoundly. He has since become extremely quiet and withdrawn.

Among his other close friends in Indore were Sakhya Matkar, Arun and Ravi Date, Umakant Akolekar, Kinna Gokhale, Radhu Mucchal, Vishwas More, Chandrashekhar Rahtekar, Narayan Holkar, Bandu Niwsarkar, Arun Sule, Bissu Vijayvargiya, and Bal Dike. In the Army, his good friends included Major Bholanath Balgu, Major MM Bahl, Major UN Sharma, and Captain M. Krishnamurthy. At Indian Oil, he cherished friendships with Deep Bhojwani, Vijay Sahni, and Mehmood Quli Khan. From the theatre and film industry, he was close to Manohar Mhaisalkar, Arvind and Sulbha Deshpande, Vijay Kashyap, Om Puri, TS Ranga, Swaroop and Anil Khopkar, and Arun Kakde.

With Arun Date & Narayan Joshi

My parents have three children: I am the eldest, followed by my brother Amrish and sister Aparna. All three of us pursued MBA degrees and have established ourselves well in life with the blessings of our parents. Hisfamily

now has me, my son Ishan, my daughter Aishwarya, and my son in-law Shreyas Desai. My brother Amrish is now married to Shilpa and has two sons Aman and Anuj from his earlier marriage. My sister Aparna lives in London and is married to Govind (Vicky) Shahi and has a daughter Riya.

Late Shirish & Anuradha

Amrish & Shilpa

Riya, Aparna & Govind

Aishwarya and Shreyas

Anuj, Ishan & Aman

My father and I share a very special bond.I am a replica of my father in my nature, disposition, and several other facets. He proudly calls me his son and tells everyone he meets that he is now living only for me. He is anxious for me because my husband passed away untimely. In his old age, he is like a little child now, such a pale shadow of his once robust and powerful self. His love for us is not overt but very deep and silent. I can

never forget one incident from 2011 when I worked at Lavasa Corporation. There was a big event that I had organized and I had taken my parents along. They were sitting in the first row and the MC went around jovially asking questions to the audience. He had asked my father what is it that he liked most about Lavasa and my father had quickly responded 'My daughter'. It was the sweetest thing to hear.

I thank God for allowing me to have my father and my mother with me in my hard days and their sunset years.

■ ■ ■

23

Happy moments and a life of learnings

As I write this book, I have come to realize how multifaceted and versatile my father truly is. Simplicity and integrity run in his blood. In 55 years of my life, I have never heard my father or my mother speak a negative word about anyone. We were a small nuclear family who did not socialize much and lived a nice and happy life. In recent years, I've witnessed a significant change in my father. He has become a contented man with zero anger. He does not talk much and is very silent. He harbors no desire to live till the point of dependency or immobility. He is financially independent and we have a 24-hour carer who is always around him. I know his silent desire is to have been able to continue acting until the end, but his mobility issues and old age have made that impossible. When I inquire about any remaining desires he might have, he mentions just one: to see his great-grandchild from my daughter Aishwarya. He hopes to spend some time of his remaining life playing with the child

I wish to summarize learnings one can draw from his life

- Take on challenges but be ready to face setbacks.
- Failures should be treated as stepping stones to success.
- Do not invite trouble. But if in trouble, get out of it with positivity.
- Be in the moment. No regrets for the past and no anxiety about the future.
- Be fearless. Never become nervous in any adversity
- Live life on your terms but carry people along.
- Aim for perfection in whatever you do.
- Think before you act.
- Live a life of discipline
- Find contentment in life.
- No gossip or ill-talk about anyone
- Remain Positive. Count your blessings.
- Be simple. Be kind.

I asked him what his most unforgettable happy moments in life have been and he said:

1. Getting a cash prize and a book written by Lokmanya Tilak from his school, for getting 100 out of 100 marks in Mathematics in the Matriculation exam in 1949
2. The 15-day stay of Shri Pu. La. Deshpande at his home in Martand Chowk Indore in 1953
3. University Medal for standing first in MA Economics at Vikram University in 1961
4. Getting selected at Jabalpur SSB (Services Selection Board) as an Officer in the Indian Army in 1963 and being a part of the Indo-Pak war of 1965

5. Receiving personal appreciation from General Candeth for his performance in the first-ever play he did in the Army, at Udhampur in 1966
6. Receiving the job offer letter from public sector giant Indianoil for a position as Asst. Manager, after release from the Army in 1968
7. Birth of his first child Anuradha after six years of marriage in 1968
8. Joining Pandit Satyadev Dubey's Theatre unit and being selected to act in the play *Pagla Ghoda* in 1971
9. Receiving the Regional award for Best Actor for the Marathi play *Jayketu* in Nagpur in 1976
10. Receiving the Regional award for Best Actor for the Marathi play *Mahabhojan Teravyache* in 1983
11. Receiving State Award for Best Actor for the Marathi Play *Wada Chirebandi* in 1992
12. Birth of his first grandchild Aishwarya in 1993
13. Aparna finding the ideal life partner and restarting her life after the divorce in 2001
14. Lifetime achievement award by Marathi Sahitya Sabha, Indore in 2002
15. Pride of Indore award by Marathi Samaj at the hands of Manohar Joshi, CM Maharashtra in 2007.
16. Listing of daughter Anuradha amongst the top 25 powerful women in Femina for her role at Lavasa in 2010.
17. Lifetime Achievement award by Saanand Nyaas, Indore in 2015
18. Lifetime Achievement Award by Zee Marathi in

2021

19. All India Radio interview for two hours on his life on Vividhbharti, in the program called *Yaadon ke Silsile* in 2024
20. Hearing eminent people from the film industry as well as the public speak about him with so much love and respect on the occasion of his 90th birthday

Life time achievement, Zee TV

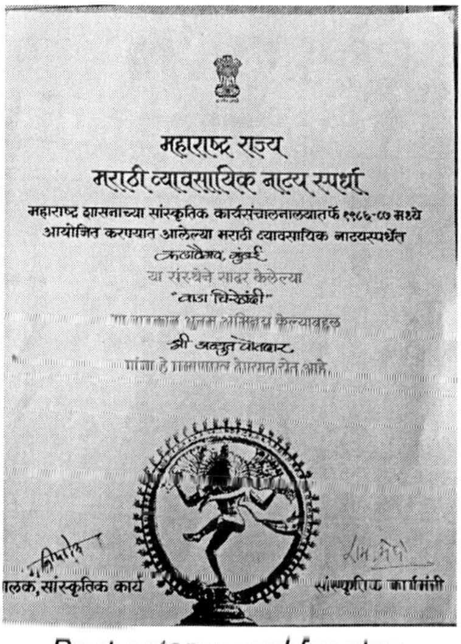
महाराष्ट्र राज्य
मराठी व्यावसायिक नाट्य स्पर्धा
महाराष्ट्र शासनाच्या सांस्कृतिक कार्यसंचालनालयातर्फे १९८६-८७ मध्ये
आयोजित करण्यात आलेल्या मराठी व्यावसायिक नाट्यस्पर्धेत

Best actor award for play
Wada Chirebandi

महाराष्ट्र राज्य नाट्य महोत्सव

Best actor award for play
Mahabhojan Terawyache

Maharashtra Times article in 2023

Lokasatta article in 2023

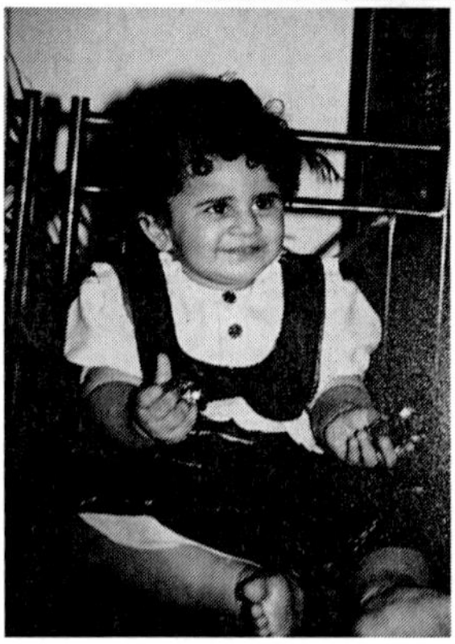

First grandchild, Aishwarya

Daughter Anuradha in Femina

Whilst these are milestone moments, my father says he has had innumerable happy moments in his life. Public appreciation of his acting skills laced with immense respect and love has been his biggest achievement he says. People still calling out *Jaggu Jaggu* or *Kehna kya Chahte ho* when they see him, or the two half-page articles on him in Maharashtra Times and Lokasatta in 2023, or the sheer comments by one and all saying what a fine and natural actor he is, have all given him*S amadhaan.* He further adds that his loving wife and the way she strongly supported him and the fact that his three children and grandchildren are solidly united, and have taken good care of his wife and him in their older age, are all good human beings, has all given him immense *Samadhaan.*

All in all, a life well lived Papa. Thank you for being you.

■ ■ ■

24

Hearts touched

I have recorded some of the admiration, love and respect that my father has garnered through his life's journey. There are many more individuals who would have liked to have expressed similar sentiments, however, unfortunately due to size limitations, I've had to limit it to just a few.

It is this love, appreciation, and respect that my father says is his greatest achievement and his biggest award in life. I could see his eyes welling up as I read out these lines and showed him a few short videos that had been sent to him for his 90th birthday

Co-actors and Directors

"There are some actors who get lost in the moment they are in the shot. Achyutji is one such actor. There is always so much belief in him, that he never hits a wrong note. Whether it is drama or comedy he is pitch-perfect. Working with Achyutji is always so much fun. He is full of zest, with a great sense of humor. Generous actor. And a wonderful human being. Achyutji, may good health always be with you. May you continue to bring joy to everyone's life. Lots of love always."

Aamir Khan

"I cherish memories of Achyut as a fellow actor during the 1969-72 period, the formative years of my theatre career. His powerful presence and resonant voice have left an indelible mark on my mind, even after three decades. Later, during my film making journey, I had the opportunity to work with Achyut again. When veteran actor Chandrakant Mandhare, then over 90, was unable to dub his own performance, Achyut generously lent his baritone voice to the character of 'Karbhari' in 'Banagarwadi', bringing the perfect depth and nuance to the role."

Amol Palekar

"You are not just a fine actor but more than that, I cherish the friendship that we have built over the last 45 years".

Govind Nihalani

"*My most favorite Papa. I think Achyutdada is the most wonderful actor, person, and screen daddy that I have worked with. I love you, Dad"*

Jackie Shroff

"I have vivid memories of Achyut ji cracking jokes with his co actors on the sets. He has always been a happy and spirited man. Whenever we worked together it was fun. I wish him good health and happiness always".

Raju Hirani

"He is incomparable. He created the character of Jaggu's father in Angaar. He wrote all the dialogues and his Ey Jaggu became so popular. Achyutji is my favorite. Unke jaisa na koi thha, na hai na hoga. He is so real. A Director's delight. I just love him"

Shashilal Nair

"Although our time working together was brief, it was impactful. Your guidance and support on set were invaluable to me. Thank you for sharing your expertise and allowing me to be part of your journey, Achyut Sir. Wishing you happiness and good health ahead. Lots of love"

Sonali Bendre

"I can't believe you are 90 today which means that when we did Parineeta you were 71. Your spirit was so youthful then and the energy was infectious. You added so much life to the sets of Parineeta in Kolkata. I remember the times you told us the military stories and also would keep us in splits so often with your witty remarks. Seeing you with your wife, made me desire to find someone in life who would partner me so lovingly. It was wonderful working with you"

Vidya Balan

"Achyut, mere dost, saari filmo mein mere saath kaam kiya hai, bhoolna mat"

Vidhu Vinod Chopra

"Achyutji is a jovial, happy person and a natural actor. I worked with him in the play Wada Chirebandi and I must admit I learned the lesser-known nuances of acting from this thespian. He is loving, affectionate, and a very helpful person. Both me and Anil respect him immensely"

Swaroop Khopkar

"Appa, as we fondly call him after the character from our serial "Majha Hoshil Na," entered our lives and we've been drawn to him ever since. It feels like we've known him forever because of the love he shares. His impeccable professionalism embarrasses us youngsters because we can't keep up with him. We feel incredibly lucky to have had the blessing of working with him."

Sujay Hande

"Our dearest Appa even at this age has so much enthusiasm, energy, positive attitude, discipline and acute love for his work. He is an ideal role model whom we can learn from"

Vidhyadhar Joshi

"A senior actor whom I had seen from childhood in serials like Bharat ek Khoj to 3 Idiots, Achyut Potdar simply became our entire unit's most loved Appa since day one. Appa kept all of us entertained and happy on the sets with his witty comments and his narration of various experiences in his acting life. Each one of us in that team can lovingly speak so much about our dear Appa that someone can ask us Kehana kya chahte ho"

Virajas Kulkarni

Family members, friends and associates

"Papa you are admired by many for the roles you've played on screen but for me, the role you played as our father in this lifetime has undoubtedly been your best! Thank you for being my biggest critic as that helped me to keep walking towards success. I love & admire you and wish you many more healthy years of peace and joy with all of us".

Amrish Potdar, Son, Thane

"Thank you and love you Papa for everything you taught me and for always being there, supporting and believing in me when I needed you the most"

Aparna Potdar, Daughter, London, UK

"Your journey, woven with wisdom and grace, is a testament to a life well-lived, reminding us all of the strength found in perseverance"

Aman Potdar, Grandson, Michigan, USA

"Papa is the simplest, clearest, most humble personality who has genuine love, care, and fondness for everyone around him. He deserves every bit of adulation and I am proud that his life journey is getting published for the world to see and read"

Shreyas Desai, Grand son in law, Mumbai

"I have fond memories of all the time we spent with Achyutrao. He has always been very affectionate and kind. Very family-oriented person. Whenever I visited India with small gifts for everyone, he would say Lilatai has arrived with her truck. I am very proud of his achievements"

Lilatai Tikekar, Wife's sister, Charlottesville USA

"Mama for me is a pure soul, all I can say is that he is made of 24-carat gold"

Vijay Kibe, Nephew, Indore

"The man with a golden heart. A sensitive and emotional human being, a family man and a perfect hero; both in reel and real life"

Mangala Kundetkar, Niece, Thane

"Mama is a disciplined and down-to-earth man. He is our guiding light and he has always supported everyone in hard times. The bond of love and affection with him has always been so strong"

Dilip Athale, Nephew, Mumbai

"A perfect hard-boiled personality. Tough and solid on the outside, emotionally soft and pure white inside".

Avinash Moghe, Nephew, Pune

"A soldier is never off duty . if this looks like just another quote, please traverse through the life of this 90 year OLD MONK "

Col. Akhil Mendhe, Nephew, Indore

"It is his military training and his passion for theatre that has kept him going so strong even today"

Bal Dike, Childhood Friend, Indore

"*Apart from being so talented He is so kind & helpful- he fulfilled a 6-year-old cancer patient's dream of meeting Salman Khan, Bhagyashree Patwardhan & Pooja Bhat when they were at the peak of their career in the early nineties. After meeting them the girl forgot all her pain of bone marrow transplant.'*

Sadhana Pawar, daughter's sister in law

"My dear friend, I remember you daily. Whenever we met in our college days, I remember how you would make us laugh. You studied so hard and secured a university medal. You were so dynamic and I was sure you would go places in your life"

Radheshyam Mucchal, Childhood Friend, Indore

"Well disciplined, full of humor and wit, warm-hearted & a very popular figure in Indian Oil. What I like most about him is his never-say-die attitude. His passion for theatre and his inherent acting prowess made even his smallest roles an indispensable part of every movie he was a part of."

Harish Bhinde, Indianoil colleague and son's father-in-law

"Achyut and I love and respect each other. We spent a lot of time together. His love for acting took him to Mumbai and am happy he could do so many roles in so many films. I am proud of my dear friend"

Vijay Sahni, Friend in Indianoil, Mumbai

"We became friends at Nagpur 51 years back. Achyut was always full of life, spreading happiness to others and making them immediately comfortable. His sincerity and ethos at the workplace were impeccable"

Mahmood Khan, Friend in Indianoil, Mumbai

"He is my guru and I have learned a lot from him. He is a man who no one can ever forget. He leaves a mark on everyone he meets. He is extraordinary!"

Vijay Sawant, Colleague and team member at Indianoil, Mumbai

"I have been his cardiologist for the last 15 years. It is a delight to have a patient like him. His implicit trust in the doctor and positive attitude inspires one to give the best to him. His meticulousness in taking his medicines is an example of the army discipline spilling onto civil life."

Dr Sandip Rane, Cardiologist

"Achyutkaka played a very big role in helping me pursue journalism in Mumbai. He and Ashatai were my second set of parents. He is so disciplined and so simple. He mentored me in the initial days of my career and I truly respect him and cherish the memories of my one-year stay with him and his family"

Lata Karandikar, best friend's daughter, Chennai

"*We have always admired Uncle's remarkable discipline and magnificent personality. As neighbors we have countless good memories that we will cherish for a lifetime*"

Archana Shah, Kandivali neighbor, Mumbai

"Mala tu awadla"... what better compliment could I get from Baba? For the world, he is a star, but I have been fortunate to get some exceptional love, sharing of memories, and friendly banter. Thank you Anu for making me and Geeta a part of your family that bonds with Baba"

Rajmohan, family friend, Hyderabad

"*Jale ko aag kehte hai, Bujhe ko raakh kehte hai, Jo gairo ko apna samjhe Unhe Achyut Potdar kehte hai*"

Shashikant, his Carer since Jan 2023

People who have never met him but admire him

" *That soulful authenticity you have built in across numerous roles, has created an indelible mark on the art of storytelling. With your boundless talent, you have lived each role that you played and carved a special place in our hearts*"

Sanjeev Prashar, Professor, IIM Raipur

"The man who triggered an iconic meme fest by rendering four words 'Kehna Kya chahte ho' in his unique style. Immortal words that will keep him and his acting legacy alive for many generations to come. A charismatic actor who infused life into sweet character roles and delivered performances that will be remembered and cherished forever."

Ashwin Shetty. PR professional, Mumbai

"Achyut Potdar as a hapless, middle-class, common man, trying his best for his family & repeatedly calling his son "Ey Jaggu", is etched in my filmy memory forever. Part shriek, part anger, part plaintive plea - it is easily one of the most forceful two-word combinations uttered in Bollywood!"

Sangraam Marathe, Businessman, UK

"A versatile actor with an x-factor, as he always leaves an indelible impression of his role irrespective of the duration - a huge asset to the film industry. I can imagine how proud the family must be of him"

Sunil Gupta, Financial Advisor, UK

"From your little biggest fan! When I was 5 years old, I loved watching you in "Majha Hoshil Na" as the coolest grandpa ever! You were so awesome, that I even started calling you my Appa at home! I love saying "Kehna Kya Chahte ho" when my parents make no sense at all"

Ronish Godambe, School student, Mumbai

"Mili's doting Rangeela daddy, to Jaggu's Angaar-bhare taunting father, to the best engineering professor at ICE. From Ardh Satya to YouTube - cheers to our most loved artist and the Youngest Monk. Here's to many more years of Rum & Fun!"

Vikrant Tayade, Media professional, Dubai

"You are an inspiration. You have strongly demonstrated how an ideal life should be. While fulfilling your duties towards the country and the family and then following your passion. Am your great admirer and a fan".

Sameer Targe, Media Business Head, Americas

"Each role he brought to life has left a lasting impression and remains close to our hearts. I love his 'kehena kya chahte ho' and I use it regularly while trying to match expressions which I never end up managing!"

Sudeep Nair, Marketing Professional, Dubai

"Baritone voice, impeccable acting, so natural an actor. I am a big fan of his and have seen all his films"

Saniraj Kyatamvar, Manager, Adani Group, Hyderabad

"I can confidently say his performances always brought smiles to viewer's faces. His talent, authenticity, and dedication have made him a beloved actor whose contributions will be remembered for years to come."-

Shreya Navelkar, Mountain Trekker, Goa.

"I frequently use his 'internet meme' which says 'Kehna Kya Chaate Ho???' to convey my point humorously and effectively during WhatsApp chat discussions! What a fine and natural actor!"

Milind Jakati, Book Editor, Goa.

■■■

25

A Comprehensive List of Works by Achyut Potdar

Films and Beyond

Hindi films

1. Ramnagari
2. Dooriyan
3. Shaayad
4. Sazza-e-maut
5. Albert pinto ko gussa kyon ata hai
6. Tum laut aao
7. Vijeta
8. Aakrosh
9. Ardh satya
10. Godam
11. Mohan joshi hazir ho
12. Giddh
13. Anant yatra
14. Party
15. Nasoor
16. Aaghat
17. Mera dharm
18. Guru
19. Kubza
20. Vardi
21. Raakh
22. Pestonjee
23. Rihayee
24. Tezaab
25. Salim Langde pe mat ro
26. Parinda
27. Narsimha
28. Disha
29. Shikari
30. Current
31. Vansh
32. Prahaar
33. Humla
34. Hasti
35. Aashiq aawara
36. Raju ban gaya gentleman
37. Chamatkaar
38. Purush

39. Geetanjali
40. Sanam
41. Aurat aurat aurat
42. Angaar
43. Bhookamp
44. Shatranj
45. Gair
46. Badmash
47. Elaan
48. Vijeta 2
49. Param vir chakra
50. Damini
51. Dilwale
52. Aandolan
53. Khuddar
54. Yeh dillagi
55. Anth
56. Udaan
57. Police wala gunda
58. Drohakaal
59. Suraksha
60. Rangeela
61. Goonda raj
62. Jiyala
63. Shastra
64. Insaaf
65. Barsat ki raat
66. Rakshak
67. Agni sakshi
68. Gambler
69. Police force
70. Yeshwant
71. Hamesha
72. Mafia
73. Bal brahmachari
74. Dahek
75. Ishq
76. Mrityu dand
77. Diljale
78. Kudrat
79. Khilona
80. Military raj
81. Khauf
82. Keemat
83. Shapath
84. Aa ab laut chalen
85. Nyaya data
86. Aakrosh 2
87. Farz
88. Vaastav
89. Yug purush
90. Daag: tha fire
91. Ham sath sath hain
92. Josh
93. Qila
94. Kaheen pyar na ho jaye
95. Ek se badh ke ek
96. Aagaaz
97. Bas intnasa khwab hai
98. Ham ho gaye aapke
99. Dil hai tumhara
100. Haan maine bhi pyar kiya
101. Bharat bhagya vidhata
102. Yeh dil
103. Rishtey
104. Dhund

105. 2.October
106. Qayamat
107. Pehchaan
108. Dev
109. Vaada
110. Parineeta
111. Lage raho Munnabhai
112. Thhodisi zindagi thodasa magic
113. Bhootnath
114. Don muthuswamy
115. Teesri aankh
116. 3 idiots
117. Lafange parinde
118. Ferrari ki sawari
119. Dabang-2
120. R rajkumar
121. Abhinaya chakra
122. 21 topon ki salami
123. Mitti ka madho
124. Chandu Gabhale
125. Ventilator

Telefilms

126. Sumi
127. Gurudakshina
128. Lalchi
129. Mukti
130. Asa hi ek warasdar
131. Sar aakhon par

Hindi TV serials

1. Dekho Magar Pyar Se
2. Nukkad
3. Naquab
4. Raag Darbari
5. Swayam Siddha
6. Kakkaji Kahin
7. Jeewan Rekha
8. Bharat Ek Khoj
9. Mahanagar
10. Kisse Miya Bibi Ke
11. Wagle Ki Duniya
12. Tenali Ram
13. Dane Anaar Ke
14. Yeh Duniya Gazab Ki
15. Upannyas
16. Mriganayani
17. Aathwa Rang
18. Faasla
19. Dhoop Chaon
20. Commander
21. Parampara
22. Dard
23. Taak Jhaak
24. Saptarshi
25. Shaadi ya...
26. Indradhanushya
27. Aasman Se Aage
28. Sab Chalta Hai
29. Nateeja thunthun Gopal
30. Sab Golmal Hai
31. Zamana Badal Gaya
32. Charitra

33. Tajurbe
34. Viraasat
35. Daraar
36. Arzoo
37. Chandrakanta
38. Faasle
39. Waqt ki Raftaar
40. Duniya
41. Kaal Kothri
42. Jeewan Rekha (Lifeline)
43. Aahat
44. Marshal
45. Sea Hawks
46. All The Best
47. Mahayagya
48. Adhikar
49. Khamoshi
50. Zee Horror Show
51. Drishtant
52. Chhotisi Baat
53. Andaaz
54. Aur Bhi hain Rahen
55. Thoda Hai Thode Ki Zaroorat Hai
56. Anhonee
57. Intezar Aur Sahi
58. Rishtey
59. Sunehare Sapne
60. Palchhin
61. C.I.D
62. Colgate Top Ten
63. Lekin wo Sach Tha
64. Aparajita
65. Pratighat
66. Daayre
67. Sparsh
68. Suraag
69. Ehsaas
70. Ret Ka Dariya
71. Eeena Meena Deeka
72. Tum Pukar Lo
73. D-line
74. Shree 420
75. Shaka Laka Boom Boom
76. Pradhan Mantri
77. Aap Haa Kahe To Haa Na Kahe To Na
78. Shubh Mangal Savadhan
79. Sponsons Top Ten(count down show)
80. Kya Haadsa Kya Haqueekat
81. Kahani Ghar Ghar Ki
82. Kaavyanjali
83. Time Bomb
84. Thodisi Zameen Thodasa Aasman
85. Viruddha
86. Agle Janam Mohe Bitiya Hi Kijo
87. Adaalat
88. Mrs Tendulkar
89. X-zone
90. Amita Ka Amit
91. Gustakhi Dil

Marathi Serials

1. Shodh
2. Gavakadlya Goshti
3. Manuskicha Gahivar
4. Faster Fene
5. Guinea Pig
6. Shortcut
7. Madhyam Madhyam
8. Odh
9. Nishpaap
10. Aawaz
11. Bolacheech Kadhi
12. Kumpana Palikadle Shet
13. Mai marathi
14. Mahashweta
15. Bandini
16. Imarat
17. Savli
18. Ghe Bharari
19. Radha Hee Bawari
20. Uncha Maza Zhoka
21. Maza Hoshil Na

Stage plays (amateur in Indore)

1. Simhagad
2. Manohar's play
3. Baba Dike's play
4. Ramesh Mehta's play

Marathi Stage Plays – From 1970

1. Pagla Ghoda
2. Suryastchya Antim Kirnapasun...
3. Aapula Thavo Na Sandita
4. JayaKetu
5. Eka Gharat Hoti
6. Graduate
7. Teertha Roop Papa
8. Mithu Mithu Popat
9. Raktapushpa
10. Yakrut
11. Mahabhojan Teravyache
12. Arya Chanakya
13. Wada Chirebandi
14. Dr. Huddar
15. Samrajya

Hindi Stage Plays – From 1970

1. Udvasta Dharamshala
2. Ool Julool
3. Abe Bewkoof
4. Aur Tota Bole
5. Kavi Kahini
6. Steel Frame
7. Sakharam Binder

TV Plays/Skits on Doordarshan 2

1. Raktabeej
2. Kamgar vishwa

3. Char divas
4. Gajra
5. Sansar sukhacha
6. Gangrene
7. Birbal
8. Tuition
9. Daakghar
10. Manini
11. Wada Chirebandi
12. Birhad Bajle

Radio (AIR)

1. Vishesh Geetganga
2. Jayamala
3. Kal ki baten
4. Celluloid ke sitare
5. VV Yaadon ka silsila

Documentaries

1. Cancer documentary
2. Udbhav documentary
3. LPG safety documentary
4. LPG safety - a talk
5. Eggs- documentary
6. Nicotinil documentary

Ad-films

1. Bajaj Scooters
2. Usha fans
3. Sainath transport
4. Family planning
5. Eveready battery
6. Vivo tonic
7. Coldarin
8. L.I.C (mangalsutra)
9. Scholar diaries
10. SBI (loan refund)
11. Bandhan oil
12. Kusum ki kahani
13. Ariel washing powder
14. Aspro
15. Rainbow sarees
16. Mili tea
17. Aaj tak's promos (elections etc)
18. Eicher tractor
19. Parachute oil
20. Sunfill (soft drink)
21. Fevicol
22. McDonald's McCurry
23. Playwin lottery
24. Sharm karo(eve teasing)
25. Sharm karo(smoking)
26. Sharm karo(corrupt traffic police)
27. AV tea
28. Saffola oil
29. Moov (family pack)
30. Maggi noodles
31. Goodday biscuits
32. HDFC (housing loan)
33. Kissan tomato ketchup

34. Travisol (Throat care tablet)
35. Dabur chawanprash junior
36. Fair&Lovely cream
37. Jago grahak jago (RBI film)
38. ICICI bank(housing loan)
39. Parachute oil
40. SBI (Dadaji ki ghadi)
41. Eveready battery
42. Sandhi amrit (tellyshopping film)
43. Bye bye piles
44. Reach tooth brush
45. PayTm
46. Entero Medicals
47. IPL Jio (Dhun Dhunadhun)

About the Author

Anuradha Paraskar is a marketing and branding professional who currently serves as an independent director on the Board of Governors at IIM Raipur. With an MBA and over 34 years of work experience, she has undertaken several leadership roles across the corporate sector, with companies like Godrej Consumer Products Ltd., Lavasa Corporation Ltd. (HCC), and the Piramal Group. She now runs her own consulting practice.

During her spare time, Anuradha enjoys painting, yoga, traveling, and writing.